influencer

influencer

Building Your Personal Brand in the Age of Social Media

Brittany Hennessy

CITADEL PRESS
Kensington Publishing Corp.
www.kensingtonbooks.com

This book is intended to provide complete and accurate information on its subject matter. However, the reader is advised and cautioned that by publishing this book, the author and publisher are not providing legal, accounting, or other professional services or advice; if any such professional services are needed, the reader should seek such services from an appropriate qualified professional.

The author has made diligent efforts to include Internet addresses that are accurate at the time of publication; however, neither the author nor the publisher is responsible for inaccurate or incomplete addresses, or for changes occurring after this book was printed and published. Moreover, the publisher and the author have no control over any such third-party Internet sites or the content contained thereon, and are not responsible for any such content.

CITADEL PRESS BOOKS are published by

Kensington Publishing Corp.
119 West 40th Street
New York, NY 10018

All Kensington titles, imprints, and distributed lines are available at special quantity discounts for bulk purchases for sales promotions, premiums, fund-raising, educational, or institutional use. Special book excerpts or customized printings can also be created to fit specific needs. For details, write or phone the office of the Kensington sales manager: Kensington Publishing Corp., 119 West 40th Street, New York, NY 10018, attn: Sales Department; phone 1-800-221-2647.

ISBN-13: 978-0-8065-3885-3
ISBN-10: 0-8065-3885-6

First trade paperback printing: August 2018

10 9 8 7 6 5 4 3 2 1

Printed in the United States of America

Library of Congress CIP data is available.

First electronic edition: August 2018

ISBN-13: 978-0-8065-3886-0
ISBN-10: 0-8065-3886-4

This book is dedicated to my husband, Alexander,
and my son, Alexander August

From sunrise to sunset I am forever grateful
to be your wife and your mother.
Thank you for believing in me and
for being a constant source of inspiration.
I love you.

Contents

Preface

I once paid a dog $32,000 for two Facebook posts, one Instagram post, and one tweet. It probably took his owner all of three minutes to take the photos and write the captions.

This dog just made more than $10,000 per minute. Pick someone that you think is really rich. Anyone at all. That dog still made more per minute than the person you're thinking of.

You work, at minimum, 8 hours a day, 5 days a week, 50 weeks a year, and deal with people who sometimes make you question all of your life choices. And this dog? All he had to do was sit, roll over, and smile.

I remember cutting a $100,000 check for an influencer to shoot three YouTube videos. Drafting her contract, I paused exactly three times to regain my composure; I could not believe that I was about to pay this woman six figures to put on makeup for 18 minutes. I almost asked myself, why isn't everyone an influencer?

But I already knew the answer to that: Because being an influencer is hard.

As the senior director of influencer strategy + talent partnerships at Hearst Magazines Digital Media, I cast influencers to star in co-branded campaigns for the digital versions of *Seventeen*, *Cosmopolitan*, *Elle*, *Marie Claire*, *Harper's Bazaar*, *Redbook*, *Esquire*, and more. That means it's my job to know the universe of influencers: understand their followings and engagement; recognize their aesthetic and tone of voice; be aware of who their agents are; and—and this is really important—know how easy (or not) they are to work with on a deadline. I have booked influencers for their first campaign, introduced unsigned talent to their current agents, and given them checks so large finance has called to asked if I added one zero too many (see the previous example).

You've probably scrolled through Instagram and thought to yourself, "I could totally do that," but you might not realize that there is an art and a science to becoming a full-time influencer. Sure, it may seem like life as an influencer is limited to posting photos of yourself walking down the street or holding an ice cream cone with an impeccable manicure. But in reality, you'll spend your days and nights creating content for audiences so fickle they can, and will, stop following you because you posted your Tuesday video on Wednesday. Or because they didn't like the color of your manicure in that ice cream photo. Or because—and I have seen this—you changed your eyebrows, you now look like "a weird bird," and your face makes them uncomfortable. And that's just your audience.

When you work on campaigns, you're dealing with an entirely different animal—the brand. Most brands don't know what they want, so it becomes quite the challenge to deliver "it" when you don't even know what "it" is and they can't explain it to you. But if you're going to make money creating content, you're going to need to figure that out. What you need is a translator, someone who speaks this foreign language, can read minds and decode the cryptic emails and briefs you'll receive. I volunteer as tribute.

Many people think you need to have a million followers to make good money as an influencer, but that's just not true. There are many full-time influencers with 100,000 followers who are making good money doing something they love, making us all jealous in the process. While scrolling through Instagram, I constantly see hundreds of aspiring influencers who are on the cusp of greatness, or at least financial independence, but they just need to tweak a few things here and there. I love to give people advice and figured I should put my journalism degree to use, so I decided to write this book. I was amazed something like it didn't already exist, but after dealing with influencers who demand to fly first class, you know, as if they were actual famous people, nothing really surprises me anymore.

This book was written for people who probably fall into one of three categories:

Category 1: You spend all day on Instagram and while scrolling through your feed, you can't help but critique other people's photos. You think to yourself, I *wear clothes, eat avocado toast, and like sunsets, why not me?* Well, let's start at the very beginning, because that's a very good place to start. Part 1, "Building Your Community" will help you come up with a brand name, create content worth double tapping, and show you how to maintain an engaged community.

Category 2: You have a decent amount of followers and feel like you're pretty good at this whole content thing, but can't figure out a long-term plan. In Part 2, "Packaging Your Brand," we'll talk metrics, public relations, and press kits.

Category 3: Brands have started approaching you because you either have a lot of followers or you lead a pretty interesting life. Maybe you're an expert in your field, you've created a company/product, or you're a dancer/musician/model/actress.

> Either way, when you talk, people listen, and that's what influence is all about. Part 3, "Monetizing Your Influence" will dive into fee negotiations, understanding your contract, and landing an agent. When you get your first check, I want 10 percent. I'm kidding . . . but not really.

In life you're constantly asked about your five-year plan, and this doesn't change once you become a content creator. Regardless of which category you fall into, Part 4, "Planning Your Future" will help you turn new clients into repeat clients and turn single programs into brand ambassadorships. We'll also talk about influencer collaborations and how you too can have your own makeup or fashion line.

If you're new to marketing, or the job market in general, there may be a lot of words and acronyms that you don't understand. That's why I've included a handy-dandy glossary at the end of this book. It's full of industry jargon that makes my head hurt . . . and I hear it every day. Read these words and phrases and commit them to memory, but please don't ask people to "hop on a call by EOD to discuss the brief." The lingo abuse must end somewhere.

What makes this book really special are the super-cool features like Expert Tips, where you'll hear from the best industry peeps in the business. Influencer Insights will pop up throughout the chapters to help illustrate my points with wise words from your favorite content creators. Don't Be That Girl is my absolute favorite, where I tell stories about women whose actions have made me say, "That's not how this works. That's not how any of this works." But rounding out each chapter is a real treat. Influencer Icons will profile some of the most amazing content creators in the game, women who have built brands and loyal communities that many Fortune 500 brands would kill for. We'll hear from Alyssa Bossio, Joy Cho, Sona Gasparian, Sazan Hendrix, Heidi Nazarudin, Teni Panosian, Alexandra Pereira, and Cara Santana. Their stories will leave you informed, amazed, and inspired.

By the end of this book you'll have all the tools you need to create a brand for yourself, your child, your dog, or even your badass grandma. And maybe, just maybe, we'll get to work together, and you'll request $100,000 for three YouTube videos. I'll probably roll my eyes so hard I'll have a headache for a week, but I'll give it to you, because you'll be worth it.

influencer

Introduction

Let's start with the most important questions: What exactly are influencers and why are they important? In general, an influencer is someone who has influence. I know, I know, it isn't very helpful to define a word by using the same word, but sometimes things really are that simple. Word-of-mouth marketing is nothing new, and it's probably the driving force behind most of your consumer habits, whether that's buying a product, binge-watching a show, or downloading an app.

But in today's digital world, the word "influencer" is most commonly ascribed to someone who has clout through her digital channels, or as some like to call it, "social currency." Whether she has a lot of followers or really high engagement, when she speaks, her audience listens, they act, and—most importantly to brands—they buy.

In the last few years, influencer marketing has really taken off and the term "influencer" has come to mean everyone and their literal mom who has a blog, vlog, or Instagram profile. It's been used to describe everyone and everything so often that "influencer" is practically a dirty word. That breaks my heart, because influencer marketing isn't bad, it's just misunderstood. Tragically misunderstood.

The *New York Times* published an article discussing influencers and spent roughly 1,000 words talking about Kendall Jenner, Selena Gomez, and Gigi Hadid, all people who are technically "influencers" because they have millions of followers. But really, they are A-list celebrities, which is worlds away from how we view a content creator with the same number of followers. One reason for the different perception is how they became influential. A content creator has to make videos, take photos, and create posts that make people want to trust her and see more. She has to use various marketing tactics to increase her audience size and keep her audience engaged. She must also adapt her content for each platform, because what works on YouTube will not work on Instagram. Traditional celebs become famous through their offline activities (singer/actress/athlete/model) and that influence follows them online and to every platform without them having to do much more than issue a press release with the name of their handle.

Not to take anything away from celebrities whose talent and business acumen have made them famous, but it pains me every time someone calls a celebrity an "influencer." Quite honestly, it shows a complete disregard for the very thing that makes a content creator an influencer. Authenticity is the backbone of the content these women create, and their audiences look to them for expert advice. Celebs are paid to promote alcohol companies even though they don't drink, or cars even though they don't know how to drive. A good influencer, the type you will be after reading this book, would never promote something she wouldn't organically share even if she's being paid by a brand. I've seen creators turn down $25,000 because something wasn't "on brand" for them. If that's not putting your audience above yourself, I don't know what is.

CONTENT CREATORS VS. LIFECASTERS

Influencers should really be broken out into two categories: content creators and lifecasters. Content creators are people who are creating blogs, vlogs, and Instagram photos out of thin air. Lifecasters are people who are just living their best life and you're following them because their feed exudes sheer awesomeness.

There are ten types of influencers and each one falls into either the content creator or lifecaster camp. They are:

Content Creators

1. **Blogger**—has a blog that she updates on a regular basis. She promotes her blog posts

through Facebook, Twitter, Pinterest, and Instagram.

Examples: @margoandme, @hapatime, @hangtw

2. **Vlogger**—has a YouTube channel where she posts videos. Whether she posts vlogs or tutorials, they all get shown extra love on her social channels.

   Examples: @ellarie, @sunkissalba, @alexcentomo

3. **Expert**—specializes in a particular industry, like fitness, beauty, or interior design. She may also be a blogger or vlogger, but she has the credentials and the training to back it up. Sometimes experts fall into the Lifecasters category, but since they focus so much on aesthetics and usually have high-quality photos, we're going to leave them in this category.

   Examples: @ohjoy, @justinablakely, @deepicam

4. **Animals, Toddlers, Inanimate Objects, and Memes**—pretty self-explanatory, these accounts manage to have tons of followers and create witty content without actually

being able to access the Internet, use a smartphone, or you know, type.

Examples: @jiffpom, @honesttoddler, @omgliterallydead, @beigecardigan

Lifecasters

5. **Special Talent**—a chef, dancer, comedian or other person who spends her days honing a skill. She posts about her craft and you care because she is at the top of her game and you want to come along for the ride.

   Examples: @joythebaker, @ingridsilva, @dopequeenpheebs

6. **Entrepreneur**—she started a business or a service and is giving you a behind-the-scenes look. You want her to succeed, so you follow her through the updates of product launches and business meetings she shares on her channels.

   Examples: @jessicaherrin, @alexavontobel, @zimism

7. **High-End Model**—she is just so gorgeous and so beautiful that you follow her to get your daily dose of awe. Never mind that she

is #hairgoals, #bodygoals, #squadgoals, and #couplegoals.

Examples: @marthahunt, @ashleygraham, @chaneliman

8. **Celebrity**—whether she's a musician, actress, athlete or a combination, she's world famous and you follow her because you love her.

   Examples: @issarae, @serenawilliams, @florence

9. **Notable**—she's usually a businesswoman, politician, or activist, and you're following for her front-row seat to her game-changing life.

   Examples: @badassboz, @gretchencarlson, @michelleobama

10. **Real People**—people who don't really fit into any other category on this list, but they're just posting away because that's what human beings do in 2018.

    Examples: @yourmom, @yourhighschoolBFF, @yourboyfriend

A quick note: For the purposes of this book, most of the time we'll be focusing on content creators, but if you happen to be a lifecaster, welcome! There is a lot you'll find invaluable as well. I'll also be assuming you're a woman. Not because there aren't a lot of male influencers (@iamgalla, @wallstreetpaper, @timmelideo, are just a few examples), but because 95 percent of the influencers I have booked have been women, that's who I'm talking to. But guys, welcome, welcome, welcome. Everything you'll read here will also apply to you!

WHY WOULD SOMEONE EVEN BECOME AN INFLUENCER?

Now that we've defined what an influencer is and the different types, we can dive into why people become influencers in the first place.

ADD VALUE TO YOUR CAREER

If you're an expert, special talent, or notable, having a high follower count amplifies all the work you are doing in real life. A great example is a comedian, actress, or model. She spends hours each day working on her skill and booking gigs, but she keeps being asked about her Instagram following. This is because businesses are always looking for easier, cheaper, and faster ways to market their products and services. A comedian with 100,000 followers can promote her upcoming show and increase the odds that people will buy tickets to come see her. This reduces the amount of money the comedy club has to spend on promoting the show and makes the management more likely to choose her over another comedian. Even if the other comedian is funnier. The same applies to an actress who can get the word out about her play or movie quickly and to an audience that actually cares about her work. A model has a similar situation: A casting director would love to book a model who would then post the photos from her shoot on Instagram. More people will see the clothing or beauty product, and the client gets an additional ad placement for free.

Plenty of people are upset that follower count seems to be more important than talent, but it's really about firing on all cylinders. In today's version of show business, the business part is happening online. You may not love the idea that your follower count may be seen as more important than your actual skills, but you need to adapt, because those who don't adapt won't make it very far. Working on your social presence shouldn't make you feel like you've sold out; it should make you feel like you're telling your own story online and building a community of people who want to support you. And if you can make some money partnering with brands, even better.

PROMOTE YOUR COMPANY

You had an idea and instead of just sitting on it and getting angry when someone else does it first, you acted. Congratulations, you have a business! Whether it's a product or a service, no one can buy it if they don't know about it, so you're off to the Interwebs to find some customers.

Once you've established your presence online, you can use your platform to showcase new products and services, show your followers the life behind their new favorite brand, and of course, acquire new customers. It's also helpful when reaching out to influencers for collaborations. They want to know who they are partnering with and make sure the brand's aesthetic is in line with theirs. The first thing people do when they see an ad for your company is to check out the profile, so maintaining that social channel should be a big part of your marketing plan.

As a founder of a business, you can become an influencer in your own right and this book can do double duty for you. Not only will it show you how to manage and monetize your personal profile, but you'll understand the flip side when you decide it's time to activate influencers as a marketing strategy.

MAKE MORE MONEY

For some people, creating content is more than just a hobby, it's their "side-hustle." They work during the day, but everything they do, they're doing for the 'gram. Many times these influencers start in one category, like beauty or style, and as they gain influence and start to make more money, they branch out and cover all things lifestyle.

This is the stage where you can try new things and make mistakes. Once you're on the radar of more brands and you have more followers, any changes you make will be scrutinized, and unsolicited feedback will be given. If you're lucky, this phase will only last about a year, so get all your experimentation in while you can.

QUIT YOUR JOB

Whether you are working full-time on your blog/vlog or creating your own makeup or clothing line, you have reached the promised land when you are making enough money that you can quit your job and still retain most of the comforts you previously had (steady paychecks, health insurance, savings).

It is by no means easy, the nights are long, and a big payoff isn't promised, but if you read this book, your probability of success will increase tenfold, because you'll be armed with the knowledge an insider has accumulated over the last decade and a list of mistakes to avoid like the plague. Let's get into it!

PART 1

Building Your Community

CHAPTER 1

The Feed

How do you find your voice and create great content?

Being a creator who is looking for brand partnerships is no different than being an employee who is looking for a job. People will google you before deciding to work with you, and they need to be pleased with what they find.

Head on over to Google.com and type in your first and last name. Now take a look at your search results for general, images, videos, and news. All the content on the first page should either be *created by you*, or *provided by you*.

If it doesn't look so hot, don't panic. Head on over to google.com/alert and set up an alert with your name in quotations (e.g., "Brittany Hennessy"). Every time new content with your name is indexed by Google, you'll receive an email to let you know you're on the right track.

Every three months, do a Google search and keep tabs on the progress you're making. Remember, if you're not telling your own story, someone else will tell it for you.

Sazan Hendrix (@Sazan) is a great example of someone who has her Google search results on point. Type in her name and the first page will pull up her website, Twitter, YouTube, Instagram, and LinkedIn profiles and a few interviews.

On the video tab, you'll see a link to her YouTube channel along with a bunch of videos she created. Head over to the images tab and it's gorgeous photo after gorgeous photo of Sazan with a few of her husband Stevie sprinkled in. Under news, a bunch of articles and interviews, and under shopping her business, BlessBox.

It really doesn't get better than this, folks. But the only way to dominate your search results is to create, create, create!

WHAT'S IN A NAME?

Many of you may already have a name, so you're probably side-eyeing this section hoping I don't say something that makes you want to pull out your hair and start over. I can't say that I blame you. Naming your brand may be the hardest part of becoming a content creator. Add in the fact that nothing on the Internet is ever really deleted, and the pressure is on. Now is not the time to choose a name that you will regret in six months, a year, or even five years. Vloggers have some of the best names, and by best, I mean the most ridiculous. I am looking at you, @sexypanda89. I won't name names, because I promised myself I would only call out people anonymously, but you probably can think of a few off the top of your head.

So how do you come up with a killer name? Well, that depends on who you ask. Some people invent entire brands, like Heidi Nazarudin (@theambitionista) and Charlotte Groeneveld (@thefashionguitar) or mashup names, like Brittany Xavier (@thriftsandthreads) and Jade Kendle (@lipstickncurls). Others incorporate their name, like Jessica Franklin (@heygorjess), Alyssa Bossio (@effortlyss) and Courtney Fowler (@colormecourtney). And some keep it super simple, like Iskra Lawrence (@iskra), Rachel Martino (@rachmartino), or Nichole Ciotti (@nicholeciotti).

You can make your name as simple or as complicated as you like as long as it's *easy to promote* (that means forget spelling forever like FOREVEERR, dropping the numbers, and leaving the underscores behind) and *consistent*. If your website is FlyFashionista.com, but your Instagram is @imaflyfashionistaaa and your YouTube is @flyfashionista4lyfe_, audiences and brands alike won't be able to connect all your profiles to each other. You can get away with having a website name that's different than your social media handles, but only if they're all consistent.

Teni Panosian is one of my favorite influencers. She is a true professional and is one of the best content creators out there. Her website is Remarques.com, but she's @TeniPanosian on every platform. The consistency of her social platforms was key when she changed her site from MissMaven.com to Remarques.com. She could easily set up a landing page to direct people to the new site, but changing her name on her social channels could have had terrible results. If people see an unfamiliar name in their feed, they're more likely to unfollow. It also means that any article ever written about her that linked to one of her channels would now point to a page that doesn't exist. But that didn't happen to Teni because Teni is smart. Be like Teni.

OWN IT

The first question people always ask is *Do I really need to be on every single platform?* and the answer to that is no. While I would recommend securing your preferred username on every platform so someone can't steal it, you should only be active on platforms you have plans on updating. Nothing is worse than finding a great influencer on a platform only to find out she hasn't posted anything new in three months.

That said, everyone should have an account on the big four: Facebook, Twitter, Instagram, and YouTube. You'll want an Instagram account, because it's where the majority of influencer marketing campaigns take place. YouTube is also a big market for fashion hauls and beauty tutorials and is also a great way to show advertisers your video presence. You may think you don't need Facebook or Twitter, but you would be wrong. The content you make is usually shared by brands on Facebook and Twitter, and if they can't tag you in it, you just lost a huge opportunity to pick up new followers. The biggest reason to keep an updated Facebook page is because at some point, you're going to want to get it verified. The little blue check may seem like no big deal, but if a brand you're working with also has one, Facebook will require that any influencer they work with also be verified. This is why you don't see as many influencer campaigns on Facebook as you do on Instagram, but that is changing, and you want to be ready. If you're a blogger, especially in food, home decor, and DIY, Pinterest can also be a great way to drive traffic back to your site. I've found that most clients don't ask for pins on Pinterest, and won't pay a lot for them unless you have millions of followers, but it's a good platform to join if you think you will dedicate the time to make it a success.

HOME IS WHERE YOUR BLOG IS

Blogging has come a long way from its early days of anonymous diary entries, and because it was the first medium to produce influencers, advertisers have had more time to become comfortable spending money on sponsored posts. They also love that they can easily provide feedback/edits on the content, unlike a YouTube video, and can give the influencer tracking links to see if anyone has clicked on the content or made a purchase.

Since a blog is pretty easy to set up and maintain, it's great for aspiring influencers who are testing the waters. Unlike a YouTube channel, you don't need video equipment or editing skills, and unlike Instagram you don't necessarily need to shoot your own photos. I have seen many beautiful and highly clicked on blog posts that are made with some text, a brand-provided video, and photos found on the Internet. Given how easy it is to get started it always surprises me how many vloggers are not also bloggers. Granted, creating and editing videos may leave you with little time to do anything else, but you're losing out on so many opportunities when you don't have a blog, because so many advertisers want influencers to create blog posts. Think about it: When you google a product or service, what comes up? Reviews on people's blogs. Sure, you may also see a sponsored YouTube video or a sponsored Instagram post, but advertisers can track how many people came to their site because of a specific blog post, and advertisers *love* things they can track.

You should also create a blog because you want to establish your home base on something you control. Any of these social media platforms can delete your profile at any time without warning, or prohibit you from promoting your other channels, but if audience members know your blog URL, they'll always know where to find you.

There are many, many resources available to help you set up a blog, but here's a crash course:

Step 1: Buy your domain. You can either do this on GoDaddy.com (it usually has coupon codes floating around the Internet) or directly from your host. If you're not that tech savvy, I would suggest buying your domain through your host to make your life easier.

Step 2: Set up your hosting provider. I use Bluehost.com because it's the only provider whose dashboard doesn't confuse me. It also has great customer service via chat so there's none of this waiting on the phone business when you inevitably break the code on your blog. Back up your blog. Back up your blog. Back up your blog. You will try to experiment with a new theme or plug-in and you will break your code and be shown the white screen of death. There is no reason for that heart attack. Pay the extra handful of dollars each month and let your host automatically back up your blog for you.

Step 3: Install Wordpress. I love Google and all of its products, but why anyone is blogging on a platform that isn't Wordpress is beyond me. Wordpress.com is the free version, but you can't control the back end and customize it to your needs, so I would skip it. Wordpress.org requires a host, but that's how you can upload custom themes, plug-ins, and tweak things until they are exactly how you'd like them to be. Your host should have a shortcut for installing Wordpress directly on their server. If you're not sure, ask them before you sign up.

Step 4: Install a theme and some plug-ins. Wordpress has really stepped up its game; there are tons of free themes that are absolutely gorgeous. Of course, if you find one that you absolutely love that isn't free, by all means, buy it. If you've seen a blog you like, you can head on over to one of my favorite tools, whatwpthemeisthat.com, to find out what theme the person uses. It's also a great resource to find out the plug-ins your favorite bloggers are using, or you can do a quick Google search for the best plug-ins for your type of blog. When you're buying a theme, you can also check out how many people have downloaded your theme. It is part of your brand and you don't want it to be a carbon copy of someone else's site. If you have the funds and can swing it, I would recommend hiring someone to design a theme for you. It's not a necessity, but it is definitely nice.

Step 5: Add in your social media accounts. Sometimes I will end up on an influencer's blog before seeing any of her social channels, and my favorite thing to do is to search high and low for her Instagram and/or YouTube profiles. JUST KIDDING. So many themes come with options to make these front and center. Use them. And make sure you link them to the proper account. This may seem like a no-brainer, but apparently it is not.

DON'T BE THAT GIRL

I was working on an event and I needed to find influencers to promote it. I found this one influencer who was great, so I went to check out her Instagram and got hit with the "Page Not Found" message. I went back to her blog and clicked on a different Instagram icon and got hit with the same message. I told her about it, and she told me she had changed her Instagram name but forgotten to update it, and that was the end of me trying to work with her. If you can't even manage the links on your own website, there's no way I'm going to trust you to manage a campaign. It sounds harsh, but there are millions of dollars at play here every day, and you need to always remember to put your best foot forward.

When looking at themes, the type of layout you choose really depends on your personal preference and how often you think you'll be posting. Just make sure your site looks modern. Wordpress has come a long way, and anyone can make their site look like a million bucks, so why people insist on having their sites look like they were created with duct tape and a dream is beyond me.

I love reading blogs for fun, and I recently noticed that many of my favorite sites were created by the same person, so I asked her to give five tips to aspiring creators.

EXPERT TIP

1. Have a point of view. Being unique is the only way to get ahead in the market today. You could be talking about the same subject as someone else, but your perspective is what makes you stand out and be remembered.
2. Trust your instinct and don't let social media drive your decisions. Be aware of what is happening and take it into consideration, but put your own aims and goals ahead of anything else and use your blog and social media to achieve them.
3. Content is still ~~king~~ queen. Although there are lots of different forms of it that are popular (written, video, podcasts, imagery, etc.), creating compelling content that speaks to your reader will create a bond between you. This allows you to create a community—which is different, and more important, than a following.

4. Trust your gut; however, use data to aid your decision making. We are lucky that we have the means to learn what our readers like and don't like, enabling us to tailor our product (the content) to what they want.

5. Networking online and offline helps keep a blog/brand alive. You need to have visibility in your niche in order to stay relevant and also grow.

—Chloé (@chloeadelia), founder and CEO of chloédigital, a tech support and strategic planning membership for style publishers

YOUTUBE VIDEOS

Vlogging may seem like a completely different world than blogging, but they're very similar, and many influencers who have found mega success are great both in front of the camera and behind the keyboard. While high-quality content with a point of view is also the goal, there are some unique aspects of video making that you must master.

- **Intro/Catchphrase.** This is usually the theme music followed by the "Hey guys, welcome to my channel" intro you see at the beginning of every video. This will set the tone for your channel and will immediately tell brands if your aesthetic and tone are in line with theirs. If your audience really skews in one direction (bubbly teenagers/moms/gamers) you can make an intro that is heavy on a theme. From the music, down to the fonts, go crazy with it. But if you want to cast the widest net, and make the most money, your intro and catchphrase should be simple, chic, and brand friendly. That means no cursing. Most brands are not too keen on their content running right behind your potty-mouthed intro, so make sure you'd be cool with your mom, grandma, and kindergarten teacher watching your intro and you should be in a good place.

- **Thumbnails.** These should follow the same guidelines as your intro and catchphrase. Any thumbnails that have crazy fonts, wacky colors, and special effects automatically put the influencer into the juvenile casting bucket. It's totally cool to have text on your thumbnails, especially if you want to call out something special from the video, but remember to keep it minimal and easy to read.

- **Trailer.** This may be the most important section of your YouTube channel, and it's sad to see it replaced on many channels by the latest video. Not only is it a tool to convince viewers to subscribe, but it's also a place to tell brands who you are, the content you create on your vlog, and why they should hire you. And please keep your trailer current. Some vloggers have trailers that are four years old. You look at that video and then at the other videos on their channel and you can't even tell it's the same person. Updating your trailer quarterly is best because it will be reflective of you in that moment. It would be a shame to lose out on an opportunity because you're a brunette in your trailer, even though you're a blonde now, and I was looking for blondes to dye their hair black for a campaign.

INFLUENCER INSIGHT

For me, my trailer is all about keeping it real. My YouTube channel is a place where I share relatable beauty videos and occasional travel vlogs. I think it's important to look into the camera and speak directly to the viewer. In my trailer I shared an overview of my channel and what they can expect. I end the trailer by encouraging the viewer to subscribe for more.

—@sonagasparian

INSTAGRAM

Since the majority of social branded content occurs on Instagram, this is where we are going to focus most of our energy. Of course, you can take some of these concepts and apply them to Facebook, Twitter, Pinterest, and Snapchat, but Instagram is the Coca-Cola of influencer marketing, and it isn't going anywhere.

- **Profile Picture.** Why people continue to have photos that are not of their face is something I will never understand. This is not the place for your logo. This is also not the place for your #OOTD. It is a teeny tiny little circle and people are absolutely nuts to try and cram a full-length photo into it. What influencers don't realize is that when people like me are pitching talent for a campaign, we have to make presentation decks to explain why you are the right choice. Decks are extremely visual, so when we need to quickly grab a photo of you, your profile picture should suffice. But it won't if it's of some random object, or it's so low-res that you look like a pixelated cartoon character if I need to zoom in. Your profile picture should be from the shoulders up, you should be smiling (with or without teeth), and it should be a well-lit photo. If you follow those three guidelines you'll be golden.

- **Bios: So Much to Say, So Little Space.** "Coffee drinker. Sunset Watcher. Random Song Lyric. Smiley Face, Lips, Zodiac Sign." You may think you're being witty and mysterious, but all I see is a bio with a bunch of words that isn't even saying anything. Not exactly how you want to come across.

  Bios are super simple, so I don't know why people make them so hard. "Creator of XYZ, a beauty and style site. NYC-based influencer. Name@xyzblog.com." Add in a location pin with your current city if you travel a lot and your blog/vlog or latest post in the link section and you're good to go. I know who you are, what you do, where you live, your current location, and your contact information.

And please, list your real name. Even if it's just your first name or your first and middle name. Your username twice isn't making anyone's job easier, and my presentations look silly when I have to address you by your handle on every slide because I don't know your real name.

DON'T BE THAT GIRL

A while back I spoke on a panel for aspiring influencers who want to work with brands. I asked everyone to participate in a little activity. I said, "Raise your hand if you have an Instagram profile." Obviously all of the hands went up. Then I said, "Keep your hand up if your contact information is in your bio." There were about seventy-five people in the room, and with the exception of five, every hand went down. I just looked at them and said, "So what you're telling me is you did all of this work to get noticed. I have found you, want to put you in my campaign, and there's no way to contact you? You just missed out on your big break." Jaws hit the ground, but I'm pretty sure they all went home and put their email in their bio.

But, Brittany, I have a business profile—isn't that good enough? Maybe if I'm on my phone, but most casting agents are on a computer during the day and your email won't come up on Instagram. Relying on the business profile means you are pretty confident I will find you on the website, take out my phone, look you up on there, tap the email button, and then type that email into a message on my computer. Have I done it? Of course. Do I like doing it? Absolutely not. Never do anything that makes it harder than necessary to book you for a campaign. You never know which seemingly small roadblock will be the reason why you were passed over.

- **To Tag or Not to Tag? That Is the Question.** Now that your photo and bio are in good shape, let's talk about brand integration on your feed. You might have noticed that many creators tell you to tap the photo to see what brands they are featuring. That's absolutely brilliant. When you're in the running for a campaign, a brand will want to see what content you've created with and about their competitors.

The last thing ABC brand wants to see is a post where you're talking about XYZ's mascara and saying it's THE BEST MASCARA EVER CREATED. Brands are super sensitive and they'll be offended that you don't think their mascara is the best. Insert sad emoji here. And since XYZ brand is not paying you, there also isn't any reason for all this praise on your feed. Add in a bunch of other brands, do a bag spill, and caption the photo with something like: "Just updated my makeup bag and here are some of my favorites that made the cut. What are some beauty products you can't live without?" And then tag (not mention) all the brands. They'll still get a notification that you've mentioned them, but you won't be calling out their competitor in a caption for no reason.

While I was writing this book, an invaluable button was rolled out to the Instagram community, and I knew it was going to get a whole paragraph. The archive button is your best friend and you should definitely use it. The archive button is commonly used for one of three scenarios: (1) You have a lot of photos with your significant other/best friend and you have broken up. (2) You decided to turn your personal Instagram into your professional one, you stepped up your photo game, or decided to start using a new filter so now all of your old photos look strange next to your new photos. (3) You tried something new on your feed, and for whatever reason, it completely bombed and you want it to go away. In all three of these cases you *could* just delete all the photos in question, but what if you change your mind? When creating branded content, you might also use the archive button when a campaign has ended and you want to remove the content from your feed so you don't alienate the advertiser's competitors for future projects. But you should never, ever, ever archive a photo until the flight is over. For more info on flights—what they are and how to archive branded content without getting in hot water with the advertiser—head on over to Chapter 6, "The Contract."

INFLUENCER INSIGHT

When I'm browsing through Instagram and checking out an influencer's feed, there are a few things that I look for in particular. The first thing that grabs my attention is the overall look and aesthetic of the photos. They don't need to be professionally shot, but there needs to be thought and consideration in the presentation of the images. Having a set filter or VSCO theme for all your photos isn't 100 percent necessary for a great feed, but it definitely helps!

I also look for a well-written bio. I can't stress enough that what you display here is so important! This is where you can hook people with a brief description of your feed's focus and any other facts that makes you unique. What's your story? What sets you apart? Try to condense it and put it here. I'm also looking to see where an influencer lives. Many campaigns I work on require talent from a certain city or area. If I know this right away from looking at your bio, that saves me from having to dig through your feed or blog for more information—aka a greater chance of getting booked.

Most importantly, a contact email should be listed right there in your bio. Along with your location, having an email address in your bio makes it easy for brands to reach out for partnerships.

—Barbara Baez Meister (@barbmmeister), associate manager of influencer talent, Content Studio at Hearst Magazines Digital Media

CONTENT CREATION GUIDELINES ACROSS ALL PLATFORMS

We touched a little bit on content, and there are thousands of articles that will help you figure out the right type of content for your channels. But here are five insights you should always keep in mind when you are courting brands:

- **Post Often.** When I'm scouting out a blog/vlog, the first thing I check is the date of the last blog post. And not only the last post on your homepage, but also for the category I'm casting for. If you call yourself a lifestyle influencer, but your last style post was yesterday, your last beauty post was a month ago, and your last travel post was six months ago, you're more of a style blogger in my book and will not be at the top of my list for beauty or travel campaigns. If you truly want to be seen as a lifestyle influencer, make sure you are spreading your content evenly across verticals. An editorial calendar will help you keep tabs on what you're posting and when.

INFLUENCER INSIGHT

My background is in print journalism, so I suppose editorial calendars have always been in my blood. They're great for keeping track of deadlines and content brainstorming. For This Time Tomorrow, I'll typically sit down at the very beginning of each quarter and plan out my high-level content strategy across my channels, from themes to topics, even to the type of imagery asset needed to support the posts. Then I reverse engineer all my deadlines from there, plotting out when certain content pieces need to be shot and written by, and potentially passed over to a client, if necessary, for branded/sponsored content. In a nutshell, my editorial calendar is my bible.

—@krystal_bick

- **Be Inclusive.** If you're doing a drugstore roundup, try to find your favorite product from each of the major players. If a brand sees that roundup and it includes everyone but them, they're going to be extremely salty about it, and a seemingly harmless organic post could cost you a future opportunity. Now that's not to say you have to include them for the sake of inclusion, but mindfulness is key.

  I'm pretty sure the first thing someone from a brand does when they go to your site is enter their name into the search box to see how many posts you've created about them. Unless they're not on brand for you, they shouldn't be led to a page that says, "Your search returned ZERO results." Ouch.

  If you're not sure who a brand's competitors are, take a trip to the store. They're usually fighting for shelf space with each other. If you'd rather look from the comfort of your own home, ispionage.com is a great resource. Just click on "competitor research" and type in the website of a brand. Under the competitor tab, you'll see a list that may not be 100 percent accurate, but should give you a good starting point.

- **Don't Be Negative.** Sometimes you come across a product or service that is terrible and you want to let your audience know so they won't be disappointed like you were. But there is a difference between giving your audience a heads-up and ranting like a madwoman. All that does is raise a red flag to brands because they know they could one day be subjected to a similar rant.

- **But Don't Be So Positive.** Every lipstick cannot be THE BEST LIPSTICK EVER!!! Just like every bag is not THE GREATEST BAG YOU'VE EVER SEEN!!! It's totally cool to get excited about a product or a service, but keep the Kanye caps and the exclamation points to a minimum or you'll risk sounding like a fangirl instead of the expert that you are.

- **Take It to the Next Level.** I get it. You're a style blogger so you obviously have to take photos of your clothes. Or you're a beauty vlogger so you obviously make tutorials, but variety is the spice of life. Your favorite media companies keep audiences interested by creating different types of content, and you shouldn't be any different. *But what types of content should I be creating, Brittany?* I'm glad you asked.

INFLUENCER INSIGHT

Authenticity is your only ammunition—without it, you might as well give up. People can smell bullshit a mile away, and no amount of money from a brand can cover up the stench. Every piece of content should feel as honest and real as possible. You should love your content as much as you want your followers to love it.

—@mynameisjessamyn

- There are four types of content I look for when determining how on top of her game an influencer is. Showcasing all four tells me that she has the skills to create multiple types of content, and this in turn makes her eligible for more campaigns.

1. **Photos of You.** How do you wear your hair? What's your makeup style? Do you wear mostly denim or mostly dresses? Do you exude more of a luxury vibe or are you an everyday girl? Do you look like you are trying too hard or are you comfortable in your own skin?
2. **Photos of Your Surroundings.** This includes sunsets, interiors, food, landscapes, etc. If I'm going to send you on a trip, I need to know you're capable of telling a story through a photo, even if you're not in it.
3. **Flat Lays and Bag Spills.** Showing me your #OOTD laid out on your bed, your suitcase as you're packing it, or the contents of your gym/diaper bag helps me envision the client's product on your feed.
4. **Video.** While this is significantly less important if you also have a vlog, it is 100 percent necessary if you do not. So much of the content created these days is video, and it's only becoming a bigger piece of the branded content pie. If you want to limit video content

> on your feed, then you need to go all-in on your stories. I can't cast you in a video if I don't know how you look or sound on camera, so this is a must to be considered for those campaigns.

In terms of balancing organic content and ads, I would follow the 70/30 rule. Put into practice, this means for every ten posts/photos/videos, seven of them should be organic and three can be sponsored. It may seem like you'll need to create more organic content as you book more campaigns, but that's okay. You don't want your audience to get sick of your sponsored posts. If they do, those posts won't perform as well and brands will stop booking you.

EXPERT TIP

When influencers are doing paid posts or posting their freebies, the images, captions, and hashtags all end up being similar or the same. So when I'm casting influencers, I'm more interested in how she's styling things she bought with her own money and not just the free swag she was given. Not only does that give me a better sense of her photography and composition skills, but it tells me more about her personality and brand. This person actually bought that velvet Chelsea boot or the floral maxi wrap dress because she actually, truly liked it and had to have it.

—Jada Wong (@jadawong), former senior editor, Content Studio at Hearst Magazines Digital Media

Sponsored posts should always make your audience say, "Hey! XYZ influencer partnered with XYZ brand. How cool!" Not, "Oh goodness, here goes XYZ influencer with another sponsored post." You also shouldn't say yes to every campaign that comes your way, especially if they are for similar products. Why would your audience believe you if you've tried to sell them on five different mascaras in the past month? Say yes to the things you like and would normally use if you weren't getting paid. Say no to everything else. Turning down money will be hard, but you won't regret it in the long run.

INFLUENCER INSIGHT

Be passionate about your brand and the content you are creating. It will become obvious in your art very quickly if you aren't in it for the right reasons. You have to love what you are endorsing or you will simply come across as inauthentic and your audience will disengage.

—***@reneeroaming***

INFLUENCER ICON

HEIDI NAZARUDIN

@theambitionista + theambitionista.com

Heidi Nazarudin is one of my favorite influencers, so it's only right to start off Influencer Icons with her. As the founder and blogger-in-chief at The Ambitionista, Heidi has created the go-to style site for successful and sophisticated women. She has used her influence to create Blogger Babes, a blogger network, Marque Media, a branding, design, content creation, and social media management company, and The Boss Box, a subscription box for the modern entrepreneur and corporate go-getter. Heidi's mission is to conquer the world in style, and it looks like she is well on her way.

ON BECOMING A STYLE BLOGGER . . .

I was the CEO of a Nasdaq-listed company, but I realized I needed to do something else, and resigned about ten months later. I didn't "jump" into blogging; I took baby steps. I read close to fifty fashion books on topics ranging from fashion history and fashion design to biographies of people in the fashion industry, and I also took writing classes. By the time I resigned, I had four clients who I could steadily depend on to hire me as a fashion writer, and was as fashion literate as any *Vogue* editor worth her September issue.

ON MAINTAINING THE BALANCE ON HER INSTAGRAM CHANNEL . . .

I have an 80/20 rule: 80 percent of my feed has to be organic content and 20 percent is paid content. It gets harder as I work with more brands, but I make sure whatever brand I work with is a brand I would use anyway or a brand that I know a large segment of my readership would love. For example, I collaborated with a dating app even though I won't use it (I'm in a very happy relationship), but I know for a fact a substantial part of my readership is single and they would LOVE the app, so it was an easy yes. I also have hard NOs. I do not work with any brands that promote inequality due to gender/race/skin color or sexual preference, and I do not work with brands that promote values I am against. Because of this, I have turned down five-figure deals with skin-whitening products and even a fashion brand that used a very controversial photographer, known for his abusive treatment of women, in a recent campaign.

ON PRODUCING HIGH-QUALITY CONTENT . . .

The three most important elements of great photos are storytelling and composition, high-quality equipment, and post-editing. When thinking about storytelling and composition you should be asking yourself, "What does this photo say?" or "What does my series of [Instagram] images say?" High-quality equipment can mean a good camera (I have a very basic SLR and a Samsung S8+ smartphone that takes amazing photos). And post-editing means ensuring your photos are edited for light balance and retouched for minor things. A lot of content creators filter their images to create the right mood. The only thing I would advise against is retouching so heavily you are not recognizable. It's disconcerting to your followers if they meet you in real life and you do not look like they thought you would.

ON RECENTLY SIGNING WITH AN AGENT . . .

I did not have an agent for the first five years of building my blog and just recently signed with the agent I am with now. Having a great agent is awesome, because you can bounce ideas off of him or her, and the agent can concentrate on making your ideas into concrete campaigns and reach out to brands on your behalf. But I loved the fact that I was doing fine without an agent too. I think it gives you an assurance and confidence to know that you're going to be okay no matter what. I decided to sign with my agent now because I am much too busy with my projects, and it's just so much more effective to have her doing certain things on my behalf.

ON BUILDING OUT A TEAM . . .

I have a full-time personal assistant, a social media manager, and an editor. I also have a photographer who is on retainer and helps me with visual content. And as I mentioned, I also have an agent who finds all my campaigns. I have a team now, but I was dealing with everything myself for the first four years with the exception of a virtual assistant I worked with on and off during that time. But it's nice to have help now.

ON HER MARIE CLAIRE *MALAYSIA COVER, WORKING ON KUALA LUMPUR FASHION WEEK, AND BECOMING AN INTERNATIONAL STAR . . .*

I NEVER would have aimed for a *Marie Claire* cover, and I really feel super lucky to have had that experience. I did have goals like "gain X amount of followers, work with X number of major brands, and keynote at three fashion conferences in the next X months." My team and I worked toward those goals, and when you have goals it's funny how things happen for you. Most goals are possible—but you need to be realistic about timing. It took me 18 months to work with Kuala Lumpur Fashion Week from the day I emailed them to the day I was confirmed.

When you're speaking to multiple countries and multiple demographics, make sure you have content that is unifying, but you should also have unique content that speaks to a specific group. No matter what I do, my content tends to feel motivational and uplifting. And sometimes funny. Which is all me. So all my content will be like that. And then I focus on specific groups. Maybe today it's about dealing with oily skin in Malaysia, and next week it's about dealing with Hollywood types (for my LA readers) and later I talk Eid al-Fitr preparations—because my family is Muslim and I have a lot of Muslim followers in Malaysia. I keep my content real and unified, but there is something for everyone. If you have a target audience from another country, make sure you have content for that specific audience regularly so they can relate to you in some way.

ON NETWORKING . . .

I think the key is to just be "real" and don't be afraid of what people will think. I talk to a lot of women, and a lot of time they overthink what to say to someone they want to meet. Just make eye contact, smile, and when they smile back say something nice and innocuous such as "I like your outfit" or "Your shoes are awesome." Anything really—and go from there. Online it's the same thing. Follow someone you like and start interacting. And be genuine. I never give a compliment I don't mean. And my best tip: Be helpful and give freely. It's funny how generous people become when you are generous first.

ON DEALING WITH HATERS . . .

I was being digitally bullied by someone who accused me of buying followers, and he decided to anonymously email brands that have worked with me (he actually took the time to find the contact emails of the brands I tagged in sponsored posts) and told them that I am buying followers. All fabricated and without proof, of course. My team, attorney, and even friends and family told me to take the high road and deal with this privately. But I decided to screenshot his emails and posted them on my social media accounts and essentially told him to "bring it." He sort of freaked out and contacted everyone he emailed and apologized. So I resolved this situation in about four hours after it happened. If I had gone the quiet route it could have cost me thousands in attorneys' fees, months of time, and a lot of pain and suffering.

I think bullies are cowards and can't deal when you show them you're not afraid. I learned who my real friends are, that sometimes you have to tackle things head-on, and that my followers are awesome. That particular post got 1,000 comments and some followers even posted on their feed some motivational quotes dedicated to me. It made me realize how unifying social media can be.

ON WOMEN DOMINATING INFLUENCER MARKETING AND INSTAGRAM CREATING UNREALISTIC EXPECTATIONS . . .

I think women are social creatures and form strong relationships and connections much easier than men, so it's natural that we dominate social media. I definitely think Instagram can create unrealistic expectations. I have had comments and DMs from followers telling me how my content makes them feel depressed or inadequate. So you know what I do now? I post lots of Insta stories and Facebook posts, usually unedited, about what really goes on in my life. This way, they see the prep that goes into that other Instagram post they saw, including the giant mess that is my office, the team that helps me out, and the 3 A.M. late nights. And if you read a lot of my captions, I poke fun at my images and my feed a lot. I am basically sending the message that the photos they see are just a highly curated highlight reel and it's mostly inspirational. The real me is just like most working women: working our asses off till 2 A.M. regularly, dealing with week-old laundry. And all the flawless photos are the product of a team working together and post editing. When they ask, I tell them that a photo has been retouched. I also post about the fact that I do have problems—I struggle with skin issues, weight issues, and work issues just like everyone else. And that it's okay and normal.

ON HINDSIGHT BEING 20/20 . . .

My advice to aspiring influencers is to put out amazing content but be real and honest. Perfect personas won't do anyone any good in the long run. The truth is liberating. I also wished I didn't care so much about appearing prim and proper. I am still polite, but I definitely speak more freely now, and it has really helped increase my engagement with my followers. I also wish that I had connected with more bloggers when I started out. It wasn't that I didn't want to, but I was so busy building content that I sort of just did it my way. Having friends who were also in my industry would have helped me avoid some mistakes.

CHAPTER 2

The Audience

How do you get people to follow you and engage?

When an influencer posts content, her audience listens to what she has to say, and they trust her, even if that content is sponsored. This is the main reason advertisers hire influencers: They want access to their audience. Brands spend millions of dollars each year creating and promoting advertisements that people block, skip over, or scroll right past, but when they can get their product/service in the hands of an influencer her audience takes notice. This is the very reason building your community is so important. Even if your content is excellent, if you don't have a loyal audience that enjoys the content you create, you won't be influencing anyone, and advertisers will not hire you.

Growing your audience may seem like a daunting task when you look at how many influencers have

500,000 or more followers. But remember, you don't need that many to become a full-time influencer. Some of my favorites, like @krystal_bick, @heygorjess, and @scoutthecity, were full-time influencers with a little over 100,000. We'll use that number as our guide, but any of the tactics that follow can be applied no matter how many followers you have.

THE ROAD TO 100,000 FOLLOWERS ON INSTAGRAM

STAGE 0: ZERO TO 2,499 FOLLOWERS

This is the window where you decide if becoming an influencer is for you. At this stage, you're testing whether or not you have the interest and the commitment it takes to create content on a regular schedule. Tell your family, friends, coworkers, and random people you meet you're an aspiring influencer and they should follow you on Instagram. Work on getting your blog/vlog and social content down to a science. You're not really on anyone's radar yet so you can still experiment and make mistakes until you get into a flow you're happy with. Also make sure to include your Instagram feed with a follow button on your blog. Many themes come ready to do this, but if not, you can find a plug-in that will help.

Once you feel like you've got your content schedule under control you can join one of the many Internet communities to increase your follower count and get feedback on your content. There are so many Facebook groups for influencers categorized by location, vertical (fashion, beauty, style, parenthood, food, DIY, etc.), and just general interest. Join them, introduce yourself, ask people to follow you, and ask for feedback on your content. Just make sure you check the rules of the group before promoting yourself or your work as some only allow links on certain days of the week. While you're looking for groups to join, you may come across something known as "Instagram pods." These are essentially groups of people who promise to follow each other and comment on/like each other's posts. This may seem enticing, but at the end of the day it may do more harm than good. You want followers who are engaging with your content because they actually like it, not just because you'll return the favor.

INFLUENCER INSIGHT

Sometimes people don't realize the amount of brainstorming and effort that goes on behind each post. Motivation is what gets you started. Commitment is what keeps you going.

—@tsangtastic

STAGE 1: 2,500 TO 4,999 FOLLOWERS

You might read articles that tell you to start using hashtags to gain followers right away. There are a few reasons why that's not the best approach. The first is because until you have your voice and posting schedule down to a science, there is no benefit from inviting strangers to look at your content. The second is because hashtags invite bots, and these will throw off your true follower count. The last is because early on you are more prone to hashtag abuse because you're desperately trying to increase your follower count. Once you have your voice and posting schedule down, then you can start using hashtags. And there's no reason to go crazy. Five to seven hashtags are more than enough to get the job done. Mix and match to see which hashtags get you the most followers and the most likes.

Some top hashtags for style, beauty, and travel are:

- **Style.** #style, #styleblogger, #instastyle, #igstyle, #personalstyle, #fashion, #fashionblogger, #fashionista, #instafashion, #igfashion, #OOTD, #ootdfashion, #ootdmagazine, #outfitinspo, #whatiwore, #wiw, #lotd

- **Beauty.** #beauty, #beautytutorial, #beautyjunkie, #bblogger, #instabeauty, #makeup, #makeuptutorial, #wakeupandmakeup, #makeupaddict,

#makeuplovers, #fotd, #motd, #cosmetics, #hairinspo

- **Travel.** #travel, #travelblog, #travelblogger, #travelphotography, #instatravel, #travelgram, #traveling, #travelling, #traveltheworld, #doyoutravel, #seetheworld, #wanderlust, #passionpassport, #digitalnomad, #stayandwander, #beautifuldestinations

INFLUENCER INSIGHT

The one piece of advice that I'd share is to find your "why" and stick to it. Share whatever it is that you love, are passionate about sharing, and have a fresh, unique perspective on, but always remember why you're sharing in the first place. These reasons vary and can become catalysts for shaping great content. Your why for sharing/posting will amplify your voice and shine through in your content. That's what makes this space so amazing—the myriad of different perspectives out there.

—@simplycyn

STAGE 2: 5,000 TO 9,999 FOLLOWERS

Once you're hashtagging like a pro, it's time to add on following people and liking their posts. At this stage in the game you only want to follow people who have a high probability of following you back. So I would limit it to people with similar content who have fewer followers than you do, and a few people who are at Stage 3. In terms of liking content, jump on a hashtag you use and like every piece of content that resonates with you regardless of how many followers the influencer has. The goal of the like game is to get on the radar of as many people on Instagram as possible. You'll see a lot of services that offer to follow people and like/comment on their content for you, but don't do it. It's a shortcut and all that will happen is your name will be associated with a bunch of emojis and comments like "cool pic bro."

INFLUENCER INSIGHT

I receive so many emails from people who want to start a blog because they want to earn money from it and make it their full-time job. I didn't earn an income from my blog for a year and a half after I started, but because I loved what I was writing about every day, it was much easier for me to stay motivated to continue. Make sure you really love whatever you're creating content around or you will tire out. Be really consistent, be committed, and be ready to work! It won't happen overnight, but if you aim to create content around your passion rather than what you could earn, you will be more set up for success!

—@thriftsandthreads

STAGE 3: 10,000 TO 24,999 FOLLOWERS

Congratulations! You are officially what the industry calls a "micro-influencer." In Chapter 4 we'll talk about creating a press kit and a one-sheet, and getting the word out to media outlets. At this level you can start being included in the "Instagrammers to Watch" lists you see on every website. Keep reintroducing yourself in groups, using hashtags, liking content, and following influencers smaller than you and a few from Stage 4.

INFLUENCER INSIGHT

Network!!! Networking is key for anyone who aspires to do anything. For aspiring content creators, I would say that you should definitely connect with other bloggers. Team up, and take over the world together. There is enough success out there for everyone, so why not lift everyone else up? Another key thing would be to make an effort to go to events as often as you can. That ties in with networking, but it always is good to show face. Last, think about what you want your brand identity to be. Network with others who are on brand with your brand identity.

—@tsarin

STAGE 4: 25,000 TO 49,999 FOLLOWERS

You might have appeared on a list or two and have a few small campaigns under your belt, and this is the stage where you start doing collaborations with other influencers. Collaborations will expose you to new audiences and help you pick up followers who might not have found you on their own. It will also help get new creative juices flowing because you'll be working with people who have their own way of creating content, whether that means using stop-motion photography or shooting in new and exciting places. It will also keep you connected to people. One thing I think aspiring influencers don't realize is that this business can be lonely. When your job consists of every aspect of your life being Insta-perfect, or at least seeming that way, it can be a bit much for people who aren't on the same path. Some of the most successful and happy content creators are those who bring their friends, family, and pets along for the ride.

DON'T BE THAT GIRL

It always blows my mind when I look at an influencer's feed and no matter how far down I scroll, not a single other person makes an appearance. Does she not have friends? Does she live a life of solitary confinement? Who is taking this picture if she literally never encounters another human being?

I was casting for a program and the advertiser wanted an influencer and her friend. My assistant and I stalked down dozens of profiles and not a single person had a friend on their feed. When you #SquadUp, your feed becomes less about you and how perfect your life is and more about how amazing you and your squad are. And besides, squadding up is how you get booked on group trips. It's like getting free vacations just for having friends. Who wouldn't want a piece of that?

Rene Daniella's (@ownbyfemme) feed has tons of photos of her looking gorgeous, but there are almost as many photos of her squad having a blast. It makes her look human, it makes her look fun, and it makes people want to follow her and see what she's up to. Sai De Silva (@scoutthecity) is another example. Her feed has a lot of photos of her, but her kids, London Scout and Rio Dash, really steal the show. And since her business features her kids and her kids are a part of her job, she can make money traveling the world and creating content with them. That is what I call having it all.

Looking for #couplegoals? Look no further than Michaela Wissén (@michawissen) and Riley Harper (@lifeof_riley). While I don't love his underscore, I do love the fact they they're always in each other's photos. They're a couple, so it would make sense that they're always together and appear on each other's feeds. And I've even hired them together, with Riley serving as a model and Michaela taking the photos.

If you're wondering how to squad up, the key is to connect with bloggers whose work you admire. Attend events, send them a DM, and make the effort to connect. I cofounded CreatorsCollective for this very reason: to help aspiring influencers affordably connect with fellow influencers as well as the top editors, brands, and agents in the industry. There are other conferences like BlogHer, Create & Cultivate, Beautycon, and VidCon, but they cost a pretty penny, so be sure you connect with a lot of attendees so you don't waste the opportunity or your money.

Everything's more fun when you do it with friends, and content creation is no different. Grab your squad and make some magic together.

STAGE 5: 50,000 TO 100,000 FOLLOWERS

At 50,000 you're ready to start approaching brands for campaigns. More times than not, a brand will post your content on its social media channels and your content could be exposed to hundreds of thousands, if not millions of potential followers. We'll talk about the best way to approach a brand in Chapter 4, but there are ways to get your content featured even if you're not a part of an official campaign. Hashtags can help new followers find your content; they're also a great way to get noticed by a brand. Maybelline asks followers to use "#mynyitlook" for a chance to be featured on their social channels, and Sephora uses "#sephorahaul." There are smaller brands, especially those that sell online only or don't have hundreds of stores, who rely on influencers to create content for them to post. It's actually the job of a social media editor to look at these hashtags and find the best pieces of content, so it's the perfect way for you to get discovered. But please remember to follow them as well. Nothing is more frustrating than hearing an influencer gush about how much they love a brand and then realizing they don't even follow the brand's social media accounts.

Want to collaborate with an advertiser and gain followers? Offer to run a contest or a sweepstakes for them, but make sure you know the difference. People tend to use these words interchangeably, but they're different. In a contest, each entry is viewed and judged to determine a winner based on some requirements. In a sweepstakes, a winner is chosen at random from all eligible participants. Ask your followers to tag a friend to share the prize or tag someone who would love the dress you're wearing in a post for a chance to win one. The prizes don't have to be extravagant. But they should be organic to your brand. If you're a beauty blogger, give away the latest holiday palette from your favorite brand. Is your blog all about fashion on a budget? A gift card to T.J.Maxx or Marshalls would be perfect. Don't give away items that any person on the Internet would love to win or you'll just end up with a bunch of people who followed your handle to win an iPad but don't really care about you or your content. Remember, increasing your followers is all well and good, but keeping them is most important. And the way to do that is by creating content that keeps them coming back for more.

THE COMMUNITY IS IN THE COMMENTS

We've covered content and hashtags and contests, but we cannot forget about comments. Comments are the lifeblood of content creators, and you should get your audience into the habit of commenting by asking them a question at the end of each post.

If brands see that your comments section is a positive place where people are sharing tips with each other, it makes you a really good influencer for them to collaborate with. Anyone can double tap a photo. It takes actual time and effort to write a comment. That's why I always shake my head when I see someone ask an influencer where she bought her bag or who makes her top and the commenter is met with radio silence.

Responding to comments is just as important as planning out your content for the week and making sure your feed looks just right. In the beginning it might be easy to keep on top of all of them, but as you gain popularity it becomes increasingly difficult. When that happens, take a few hours each week to go through your comments and answer all the questions and like as many comments as you can. If it's more than you can handle on your own, enlist a friend to help. If you take two seconds out of your day to interact with this follower, the odds that she will engage with future pieces of content shoots through the roof. Take care of your community and it will take care of you.

INFLUENCER INSIGHT

Answer as many comments as you can, until it becomes too much to handle. A small amount of comments can double quickly if you answer every person. By doing something that simple, you can double your engagement. It is so important to interact with your subscribers to build a relationship and a community.

—*@sonagasparian*

It's great when you receive a lot of positive comments or constructive criticism, but what about the feedback from the mean girl who could win a prize for most passive-aggressive comment? It's easy to scroll right past negative comments when you're on someone else's feed, but what do you do when those comments are about you? Many people say, "Ignore the haters," but it's easier said than done.

EXPERT TIP

One of the most common mistakes influencer talent can make is oversharing. Once you put something out there, you can't take it back. I'm not saying not to be your true self and authentic to your brand, but some things should be kept personal or it could get to a point where you no longer have control.

People will always have something to say about who you are and what you're doing. Don't feed into any of it. The more you ignore the online trolls and haters, the better off you'll be. Do what you know well and you'll succeed.

—Rana Zand (@ranaburgundy), head of talent at Authentic Talent and Literary Management

I came across a site that was so lame I will not even mention its name lest you check it out and give them page views. This site had a thread where you can praise an influencer and it had over 8,000 posts. I thought that was pretty cool until I saw there was also a thread where you could talk smack about an influencer, and it had 1,400,000 posts. Wait, what? Who are all of these people sitting around drinking cases of Haterade? Don't they have something better to do? Spoiler alert: They do not.

When you're creating great content, you will amass an audience that is living vicariously through you, but you will also pick up quite a few followers who are jealous and want to tear you down. And the bigger your audience gets, the more of a target you become. Luckily, social networks have wised up and now let you turn off comments for a particular post, or block comments that have specific words in them. Use these features and don't be afraid to delete hateful comments and block people. It's what is best for your own sanity and the community you are building.

Chances are your haters are just fans who can't express themselves in a way that makes any logical sense because there's a thin line between love and hate. When they make an appearance in your comments section, thank them for being an active member of your community and keep it moving. You don't have time for this negativity. You have moves to make.

BUYING FOLLOWERS AND LIKES

I saved this for last because, although it shouldn't need to be said, I am going to say it anyway. When it comes to buying followers and likes, don't do it. *But what about those sites that promise follows and likes from real people?* Don't do it. *But what if I get a really good deal and a recommendation from a friend?* Don't do it, and that person is not your friend. *But what about those sites that will comment on other people's photos on my behalf?* Don't do it. Don't do it. Don't do it.

DON'T BE THAT GIRL

I have a list of rising influencers that I keep an eye on. Their follower counts are small, but I know it's only a matter of time before they're players in the game because their content is really, really good. As soon as many of them hit 100k, I pounce and start pitching them for campaigns, and clients LOVE it when you show them people they've never seen before.

But there was one girl who I had been following for months. During one of my check-ins I saw that she had jumped 30,000 followers and was almost at 100K. I was super excited for her. Surely someone had also discovered this brilliant content creator and featured her on their site and that's why she had this surge in followers. Wrong. I looked at her engagement and realized it was super low for someone who had as many followers as she did, so I looked at a growth chart. And

> lo and behold, over about two weeks, her follower count skyrocketed. It became obvious that she had paid for followers. Had she just waited a few more months she would have hit that number anyway, but she cheated the system. I noticed, and I'm sure I'm not the only one. Needless to say, I didn't reach out to her and I probably never will.

You may or may not remember a little thing called the Instagram purge that happened in 2014. Instagram decided to remove all the fake accounts and bots, and celebrities and mega influencers alike had their follower counts decimated overnight. There's no telling when the next purge will happen, and you don't want to be like rapper Ma$e, who went from 1.6 million to 272,000 followers overnight. He was so embarrassed that he deleted his account. That won't happen to you because you know better. Right? Right.

If you are in this business for the right reasons, creating great content, and engaging with your audience, the followers will come. This isn't a sprint; it's a marathon. Never forget that.

INFLUENCER ICON

SAZAN HENDRIX

@sazan + sazan.me

Sazan was one of my first big "gets" when I started working at Hearst. I had been following her for quite some time, but didn't have the right campaign for her. When I needed a fashion blogger who could self-shoot monochromatic outfits for the holidays, I knew Sazan was my girl. She is lovely to work with and has one of the best squads on the Internet.

ON STARTING YOUR BLOG . . .

Before I started my blog I wish I asked myself these questions:

- Am I willing to INVEST? (time, money, and energy)
- Am I willing to RESEARCH? I've never been a good student, but blogging forced me to dedicate countless hours to research before hitting the "launch" button on my blogging career.

- Can I COMMIT? Starting a blog comes with sacrifice. I quickly learned that I had to be willing to sacrifice my time and really commit the energy to my blog—especially in the beginning.

ON LAUNCHING YOUR YOUTUBE CHANNEL . . .

Launching my YouTube channel was seriously the best decision I made during a time in my blogging career when I felt like I wanted to offer more on a personal level. Vlogging is my favorite type of video. I create vlogs (whether it's travel or personal) because I love that they're REAL. They go beyond just fashion and beauty, and allow others to feel like they can know me on some level.

ON YOUR INSTAGRAM PERSONA . . .

My Instagram "persona" has definitely evolved from pretty flat lays to real-life candid moments. I've learned what works best for me (from a content standpoint); my followers enjoy the personality-filled moments the most. I try to post based on my mood and the season of life I'm in. Life is unpredictable, so really it's impractical to strategize too far in advance; however, I do like to go through my camera roll and organize my IG feed and content through the UNUM app, which helps plan out my posts.

ON GROWING UP ONLINE . . .

I'm pretty much an open book (for the most part). The parts of my personal life I enjoy sharing are the highlight moments, or times when I feel like there's something in my heart I need to share. I've shared the good, the bad, and the ugly with my audience, and I think there's a level of respect and appreciation that I've gained by doing so. I believe it's what sets me apart from other influencers. Negative comments used to get me down (I'm human!), but after a while I realized that it's not me they have an issue with—it's something within themselves that they are projecting onto others. I try to ignore it or kill it with kindness. :)

ON BUILDING YOUR SQUAD . . .

The blogging community is amazing—especially when you find girls in your profession who you can relate to on a personal level. I definitely think it's important to have friends on the same/similar career path. You can help, encourage, motivate, and teach each other your ways! I don't know where I'd be without my girls.

ON STAYING AN INDEPENDENT . . .

I quickly learned early on that an agent just wasn't for me. I am super hands-on and have an amazing internal team that I've personally scouted and built. As of the past year, I brought on a personal manager, Barrett Wissman, who works closely with me and just a few other clients. My hairdresser is the one who introduced us, and ever since we've had him on board, he has taken my career to the next level. Thanks to him, we brainstormed and executed my second business venture, called the Bless Box. It's really amazing when you find the right person who sees your vision and works just as hard as you to make it a reality.

ON KEEPING IT IN THE FAMILY . . .

I can't work with people who I don't trust, so for me working with family was GOALS! Stevie (my husband), Brittany (my sister-in-law), and I noticed how well we all worked together and decided to really focus and take this business to some serious heights. We all know our roles and do such an amazing job owning that role. We all love our jobs, and truthfully, it's a blessing being able to run a blogging business that can financially support us all full-time. We rarely fight, but when we disagree, we never let that come between our personal relationships with each other. Work is work and that's how we look at it.

ON GIVING BACK . . .

I 100 percent believe that digital influencers have the platform, talent, and capabilities to create content that goes beyond our "brands." It's amazing how we can influence people in a positive way through the Internet and social media. When I launched Bless Box, my subscription beauty box, I always had a vision to take it a step further and launch the Bless Gives Back Initiative. I love people, and truthfully just felt like I could be doing more in my community to help others in need. I was amazed by all the love and support we received for the launch, and the highlight for me was getting to team up with Lauren Bushnell, one of my digital influencer besties, and surprise kids at Vista Del Mar [a treatment center for children with disabilities, located in Los Angeles] with a visit! It was such an amazing day.

ON WOMEN DOMINATING INFLUENCER MARKETING . . .

Who runs the world? GIRLS! As a girl boss, I think it's really awesome that we've paved the way for young girls who want to get into this new industry. I can't speak for everyone, but I can say: the more real I've been with my online persona, the more I've connected to women all around the world. My advice to young girls is to BE YOU. Embrace your quirky side or that special thing about you that makes you, well—YOU.

ON HINDSIGHT BEING 20/20 . . .

I wish someone had told me when I started that it's okay to not have everything figured out in the beginning. I used to think I had to have it all mapped out. The truth is, you have to find comfort in discomfort in this space, knowing that it's fast-paced and always changing. Change is good, and you can't let it slow you down from your "end game" goal. Embrace change and all the growing pains that will come with it.

PART 2

Packaging Your Brand

CHAPTER 3

The Edge

How do you stand out from the crowd?

There are a lot of aspiring influencers, and if you want to work with the best brands you'll need to stand out. Whether it's understanding your audience engagement and demographics, possessing special skills, or producing high-quality content, the more you bring to the table, the higher your chance of being booked and being paid well.

E IS FOR ENGAGEMENT

The first question a brand will ask about an influencer is, "How many followers does she have?" The second question is, "What's her engagement rate?" What they're really asking is, of all of your followers, how many of them are actually liking and/or commenting on your content?

Whether someone is clicking a heart or the thumbs up, sharing, retweeting, or taking the time to comment, this all means they are actively engaged and interested in what you are posting. Each platform has its own system, but it all means the same thing: engagement!

Instagram	**YouTube**	**Facebook**	**Blog**
Likes + Comments	Thumbs Up/Down + Comments	Likes + Comments + Shares	Comments

Here's the formula to determine your engagement rate for a particular post.

[Likes + Comments] ÷ Followers (at the time of the post) = Engagement Rate

For a more holistic engagement rate, you can find the average number of likes and comments for a particular month, but I generally use the last ten posts. There are also plenty of websites that will calculate this for you for free like influencermarketinghub.com.

A decent engagement rate is 1.5 percent to ~2.5 percent, but your goal should be to exceed 3 percent. Sometimes your overall engagement is important, but other times I might need a more targeted snapshot. For instance, I may just calculate the engagement on your Instagram videos. Or if you're primarily a beauty influencer who also posts about style and travel, I might only look at the engagement on your beauty posts because that's the main reason your audience follows you. But all other things being equal, I always book the influencer with the higher engagement because it shows the audience will actually respond to and interact with her content. And that's the entire reason I am paying her.

A/S/L

After knowing your engagement rate, the next set of numbers to know are your audience demographics. The big three are age, sex, and location (A/S/L). Some things never change.

1. **Age.** The age of an influencer doesn't always dictate the age of the audience. If your content is bright, bubbly, and focused on DIY, your audience might be teenagers even if you're thirty-five. On the flip side, if you're a twenty-year-old mom blogging about raising twins, a majority of your audience will probably be much older than you are.

2. **Sex.** Influencers who tend to show a lot of skin usually have a lot of followers of the opposite sex. If a brand is trying to promote a new lipstick, and all your followers are men, you're not the best fit. But what if a brand was trying to promote a

new beer, or some other gender-neutral-but-skews-male product? Well, then, you would be the best girl for the job.

3. **Location.** This really comes into play for events and special rollouts. I do a lot of campaigns for a luxury mall in California, and they want the influencer's audience to live close to their locations. Another case is a product that's only available in certain markets. If you can show me that your audience lives in one of those markets, you're hired.

How can you figure out your demographics? On a blog or your YouTube channel, Google Analytics will be your best friend. The easiest way to see your demo numbers on Instagram is to sign up for a business account. (It used to be controversial to switch to a business account because Instagram was still working out the algorithm and a lot of people's engagement dropped. It's leveled out, so it's safe to do so now.) There are also websites like hyprbrands.com that will let you run a free search and pull more detailed information on your audience. They can offer these free services because they make their money from brands that need to run hundreds of these reports when putting together a campaign roster, so it's definitely a tool you should take advantage of. Some of them even show breakdowns of your audience by ethnicity and household income. This last one is a great figure to have if you want to pitch luxury brands. You can prove to them that your audience can afford to buy their product.

BRANDS ONLY LIKE INFLUENCERS WHO HAVE GREAT SKILLS

Skills are important, so you need to spend time and effort honing them. Knowing how to pose for a photographer, speak on camera, and work the red carpet are skills every successful influencer must have.

YOU BETTER WORK

One of the trickiest things about booking an influencer for a photoshoot is you don't know if they can perform when it's not their personal photographer behind the camera. Sure, your boyfriend can follow you around all day and snap hundreds of photos until you find a few you like, but we don't have that luxury during a campaign. We sometimes have to shoot ten looks during one shoot and we don't have all day, so we need the influencer to bring it for every single shot. Now, you don't need to be a professional model, but when there is a room full of people ready to take your photo, you need to know what to do. Here are some tips:

- **Learn to take direction.** Many influencers have photographers who can take decent photos, but they usually don't give them directions to follow. On set you'll need to do more than turn left and turn right. Laughing on cue and being able to repeat the same motion in different ways are two of the big ones. I once saw @alexcentomo step out of a tent twenty times, and each time she did it in a different way. Needless to say, she is one of my favorites.

- **Know how to sell a product.** The reason you are in this branded content piece is because an advertiser has paid you to help sell its product. If it's a campaign for a handbag, you need to know how to bring that handbag to life by interacting with it in different ways. If it's a beauty product, you'll need to learn to purse your lips and bat your eyelashes in a way that makes the lipstick or mascara pop.

- **Have a go-to look.** Every model has that one look that they're known for. Practice one really great face and body pose that you can whip out in a pinch.

- **But don't limit yourself to that one look.** There are so many influencers who make the same face in every photo. That may work for your Instagram, but it doesn't work on a professional shoot. You need to know how to look elated, surprised, ecstatic, overjoyed, and other variations of happy. But those faces need to look different and not like Blue Steel, Ferrari, Le Tigre, and Magnum, which are all pretty much the same look. Okay, they're exactly the same look.

- **Lose the accessories.** I once worked with an influencer who didn't want to take off her sunglasses. No ma'am, that is not going to work here. Now, she had a very prominent nose, and this was how she felt comfortable disguising it. I'm all for anything that makes a woman feel more comfortable in her own skin, and it wasn't the worst thing because we shot most of the images outside and during the daytime, but what if the concept was a dinner party? Was she really going to wear her sunglasses inside and at night?

- **Relax on the photo editing.** I understand there are apps that can slim your face, clear your skin, make your eyes brighter, and plump your lips, but all this editing can make you look like someone else. Sure your photos will look great and consistent, but the last thing you want when you show up on set is for everyone to wonder when the influencer they hired will be arriving.

EXPERT TIP

Often the makeup looks we shoot for branded campaigns are different (more natural) from Instagram makeup looks, which tend to be more dramatic and filtered. I would advise beauty influencers to show a variety of natural, unfiltered snaps on their IGs so that editors/brands have a true idea of their versatility and look. There's nothing more frustrating for an editor/brand than when an influencer shows up on set looking dramatically different in person than they do on their Instagram feed. Giving an accurate representation of who you are is the best way to guarantee more work.

—Jennifer Tzeses (@jtzeses), former beauty director, Content Studio at Hearst Magazines Digital Media

LIGHTS, CAMERA, ACTION

Teni Panosian, Sona Gasparian, and Jenn Im are three of the best influencers to cast for a video campaign because they all are excellent on camera. Is it a coincidence that they are all YouTubers? I don't think so. As I mentioned in Chapter 1, even if you're a blogger with a great Instagram, you should still have a presence on YouTube. Even a channel with 1,000 followers will allow you to: (1) get comfortable in front of the camera, (2) create videos to add into your blog posts for campaigns, and (3) have some examples of your video presence for casting directors to view.

But all YouTube experience is not created equal. There are plenty of YouTubers with 1MM+ followers who are not the best fit for campaigns. Sure, they can vlog, but if you take them out of the comfort of their bedroom, their entire persona falls apart. Video shoots are very similar to fashion shoots, in that you'll need to know how to be "on" at the drop of a hat. The way to bring your best self to a video set is to focus on these three areas:

- **Scripts.** When you're creating a branded content video, there are key points the advertiser wants to come across, but you shouldn't read the script word for word or you'll sound like a terrible car commercial. Practice by going on a website for a clothing company or beauty company and reading the descriptions of products and then rereading them right after in your own words.

- **Body Language.** For most beauty and hair videos, you'll be sitting in a chair looking right at the camera while you use the product. You don't want to look stiff or uptight, but you also don't want to look sloppy. Practice by reading while looking in a mirror. Little things like arching your eyebrow, tilting your head to the side, and waving at the open and close of a video can be the difference between a video that is boring and a video that is super engaging.

- **Filler Words.** Nothing slows a video down faster than "um," "like," and "you know." This is another one of those things that may fly on your YouTube channel but will not work if you're going to make branded videos. Most web videos are 30 to 60 seconds, and you can't waste precious time with nonwords. If you're guilty of this, practice, practice, and practice some more. When you can speak on a subject for 60 seconds without using any of those nonwords, you're ready.

AND WE'RE LIVE

One of the biggest trends is using influencers to cover events and then streaming that coverage via Facebook Live. To be great at this, you'll need all the skills listed previously and then some. This is an area where you may need to initially offer up the goods for free so you can put together a reel and then start charging for your services. We'll talk about how to land those gigs in Chapter 4. But first, here are three things you need to remember when you're covering a live event:

1. **Do your research.** You should be combing the Internet in preparation for the big event. If you're interviewing a designer, you shouldn't ask him to tell you about the collection. Dozens of people have already asked that question. Take that knowledge and spin it into a better question like, "You say this collection was inspired by your muse XYZ celeb. What qualities do you admire about her and how did those inform the design process?" Much better question.

2. **Dress appropriately.** Of course you want to look camera-ready, but you also need to be comfortable. Shoes that hurt your feet or dresses you cannot breathe in

will not do. Ditto for clothing you constantly need to adjust, like skirts that ride up and shirts that slide forward. If you are uncomfortable, it will change your mood, and you will be a bad host for the evening.

3. **Remember, it's not about you.** You see this all the time when watching celebrity YouTube collaborations. There are influencers who understand they're supposed to interact with the celeb and bring value to their audiences. Then there are influencers who think they ARE the celebs and are completely rude and unprofessional. That is the quickest way to be blacklisted and never invited to work with a brand ever again.

PRODUCTION MATTERS

All the tips so far have focused on being on set for a campaign. But how do you develop an edge when an advertiser sends you products and wants you to create content around them? One word: production.

Let's say you are doing an organic roundup of your favorite bath products for your blog. You might take some great photos in your bathroom and call it a day.

But if you're doing branded content, and I just gave you $5,000 to do a photoshoot with my product and post an Instagram photo, you better not even THINK about shooting it in your bathroom. I'm pretty sure $5,000 can buy you one night at the nicest hotel in your city, a professional photographer who will bring his own lighting, and a photo editor who can make the advertiser's products and your skin look amazing. You have a budget because the brand wanted you to step up your game and produce a shoot.

The ability to deliver great content that can be dropped right onto a website or into a magazine is what separates the good influencers from the great influencers and gets you the highly coveted repeat business.

EXPERT TIP

When you're booked for a campaign, first and foremost be grateful. Influencers are a dime a dozen these days, and you'd be wise to remember that you're not the only fish in the sea.

If and when you are booked, set yourself apart from the rest by delivering several more assets—be it images, quotes, etc.—than you're contractually obligated to provide. It proves you're flexible, easy to work with, and dedicated to ensuring the editors and brand have more than enough options to work with in order to make the content/feature phenomenal.

Another pro tip? Read the brand's correspondence carefully, so you can respond accordingly and promptly. Whether you're in the early stages of negotiation, or handing off final assets, make sure you and/or your manager are swift and succinct with replies. Time is money—literally.

—India-Jewel Jackson (@indiajeweljax), former style director, Content Studio at Hearst Magazines Digital Media

When producing content, the most important thing is location, location, location. If a brand is asking you to style a jacket five ways, you'll also need five very different locations to make sure each look is fresh and can pique your audience's interest.

When you're picking a photographer, find those who can shoot outside in natural light, but can also shoot indoors. If you're showing how to wear a look for date night, you can't shoot ALL of your photos outdoors, because most dates take place inside. I have given influencers product to shoot indoors, and the photos have come back absolutely terrible because their photographer didn't know how to light a room. You may not need that much range for your personal feed, but like I said, producing branded content is a different game. If your personal photographer doesn't know how to shoot in different environments, hire one who does.

EXPERT TIP

When I receive a new project, five ideal locations usually come to mind within seconds after reading the creative brief. The key to a successful photoshoot is scouting your location beforehand and mapping out your shots to maximize your time. The most important element in creating a beautiful image is lighting. Most people instantly look for the right decor or space size when scouting. What they should be looking for is light and how it will be hitting the subject. Be sure to scout a location during the same time frame as you would be conducting your photoshoot. Light changes minute by minute.

—Hannah Kluckhohn (@hkluck), photo producer, Content Studio at Hearst Magazines Digital Media

And don't think you can stroll into any location and just start snapping away. Usually, you'll need permission.

If you're in a small town you might be able to get away with it, but you're going to need assistance if you live in New York, Los Angeles, Miami, Chicago, and other big cities. This is where publicists come in. Their job is to secure placements for their clients—restaurants, hotels, etc.—and if you have a great feed they may want to partner with you. What better way for the venue to get free exposure than to be in an influencer post? Of course, the influencer must be in line with their brand, so they are selective. Publicists cover every vertical, so the more publicists you know, the more access you'll have to hotels, restaurants, museums, and other cool places they represent.

Interesting locations, stellar engagement, and a great on-camera presence are all things that will help you stand out from the crowd, but at the end of the day, knowing who you are, what makes you different, and channeling that, is what will really give you an edge.

INFLUENCER INSIGHT

The industry is saturated. After a while, every hundred bloggers start looking the same. Your superpower is being you. Use it to your advantage.

—*@thegreylayers*

INFLUENCER ICON

ALYSSA BOSSIO

@effortlyss + effortlyss.com

When I met Alyssa I was completely blown away by her drive and level of professionalism. She is constantly pushing her brand to the next level, and it shouldn't surprise anyone that she graduated from college and became a full-time influencer. Her audience looks up to her and flocks to her meet and greets for an in-person dose of her positivity. On her Instagram feed you'll find her standing on the edge of cliffs to get the perfect shot. She's giving her audience everything she has, and they are loving it.

ON BECOMING AN INFLUENCER . . .

I knew I always wanted to do something "different," but I never knew what because I had so many different passions. I was always interested in the Internet and social media. I was the first one of my friends to have AOL, an email, and a screen name, and I was the first to have Myspace, then Facebook, etc.

I was always using different platforms and experimenting, and I loved it. I didn't have to convince my parents to let me pursue it, but they were definitely skeptical! They believed in me all along, but they were pretty surprised when they saw me move out and be able to afford living on my own.

ON PIVOTING FROM FITNESS TO LIFESTYLE AND TRAVEL . . .

I knew I needed to change my overall "direction" because I wasn't satisfied limiting myself to one particular niche like fitness. I love working out, it's great and makes me feel amazing, but I truly wasn't happy only posting fitness-related content. It also made it more difficult to work with brands that weren't fitness related. So, I decided to transition and slowly incorporate more lifestyle and travel content. I was fortunate enough to have high engagement on those photos, and my audience seemed to love it. Most people were supportive of seeing more high-quality content. Some unfollowed me, but more new people followed me!

ON PRODUCING HIGH-QUALITY CONTENT . . .

A lot of different components go into high-quality content. I plan my outfits, my hair, and my makeup to start. Then, I have to scout out a good location where not a lot of people have been before, or just a really scenic spot that will look the best for the shot. I also had to invest in a good camera, several different lenses, and editing software to make every photo unique and different. And there's not much of a difference between organic content and brand content; I try to make all of my photos as creative as possible, regardless if I'm being paid or not.

ON TRAVELING SO OFTEN . . .

I have a lot of cozy clothes for airplanes, and I stay as hydrated as possible when traveling! It's actually nice to be able to travel all the time, but it does definitely take a toll on my energy levels and my health at times. Traveling inspires me the most, so I wind up creating a ton of content. I lose a lot of sleep staying up to shoot and edit everything.

ON BUILDING A POSITIVE AND ENGAGED COMMUNITY . . .

I used to delete any hateful comments, and now it's gotten to the point where not many people follow me to hate on me. I think the bigger you grow your brand, the more hate you will receive, but I've been lucky enough to grow an overall supportive audience. I do still get some hateful messages, but I ignore all of that now.

I think it's just important to be real and to interact with your audience as much as possible to show them you care that they follow you. I message a lot of them randomly, answer their questions, and reply to nearly all of my photo comments. I also make sure my content is always true to my brand, and I am EXTREMELY selective with my partnerships. I don't post ads on a daily basis for a reason. It looks tacky, and I always want to be true to myself. Meet and greets are another awesome way to connect and make new friends. I think everyone should do them, even if they have a small following.

ON WORKING WITH YOUR SIGNIFICANT OTHER . . .

My boyfriend is also my photographer, but that decision was not an overnight one! We actually dated for a full year before deciding to jump on board together and take that step. I think it's hard to work with someone you are dating, and if you decide to do that, make sure you're always on the same page and you are both level-headed when it comes to making business decisions. I also think it's super important to separate business from personal issues, so you have to learn how to do that. It's not as "couple goals" as it seems!

ON WOMEN DOMINATING INFLUENCER MARKETING . . .

I think women deserve to ask for the fees if they work hard. Women are driving this market because we have built strong brands with strong audiences that listen to us, and that drives an amazing return on investment for brands that want to work with us. We are the new faces of digital marketing, and we have the power to influence thousands of people, and that's extremely valuable at this time.

Building a digital brand is not an easy process, and takes a lot of work, time, and creativity. I've worked extremely hard to build myself up to where I am today. I didn't wake up with a million followers overnight—it took seven years. I've been through the process of people saying no to me a thousand times, looking down on me, brands constantly rejecting me and my work, etc.

I would tell young girls who want to do this job to really think about what is going to differentiate them from everyone else and be true to their actual personality and content. I see a lot of girls trying to get into this world now, and they're all copying each other's exact photos and replicating things, which isn't going to propel a brand much further. You have to stand out and show people why you are truly unique!

ON HINDSIGHT BEING 20/20 . . .

I wish I knew not to listen to anyone who told me social media wasn't a real job! I doubted myself more than I should have. Now I know that if you work hard at it, anything can turn into your full-time job! Also, just be patient with the process of learning how to create content, edit, shoot, etc. Over time, you will learn the ropes and get better and better at it, just like anything else. Looking back at my old photos, I see how far I've come with creating content and building an audience, and it's amazing to go through that learning process.

CHAPTER 4

The Press

How do you get sites and brands to notice you?

Before you start putting yourself out there for everyone to see, you'll need to make sure your digital house is in order. Whenever you reach out to someone, or if your name comes across their inbox, the first thing they will do is google you. As I said in Chapter 1, one of your first search results should be your website, and it's really important that your site is top-notch. When someone is casting for a campaign, the pages of your site are where they are going to find all the information that makes them want to hire you. Three simple pages can be the difference between getting hired and getting passed over.

SO, TELL ME ABOUT YOURSELF

You need to make sure you have both an "about" and "partnership" page, and these pages are crucial. This is where I want you to tell me everything I could possibly want to know about you. And I mean everything. This is a real request I've gotten:

> *We're looking for a female musician who is from New York, but now lives in LA. In a perfect world, she has a dog and is vegan.*

Pretty detailed right? Now for comparison, the typical bio looks like this:

> *XYZ influencer is a lover of fashion, dogs and wine. She started blogging as a hobby and has turned it into a full-time career. She wants everyone to know they are beautiful and can have great style on a budget.*

UGH. Insert face palm emoji here. This person could totally be who I'm looking for, but she could also be completely wrong for the campaign. I check out her site a little more and see that she has a partnership page, so I go check it out. It's just a bunch of logos from past partnerships she's done. Sigh. So, I still don't know if she's right or not. In a perfect world it would be set up like this:

ABOUT PAGE

- **Nice hi-res photo of your face.** As stated in Chapter 2, when I pitch influencers to companies, I almost always have to make a deck. I'll need a photo of you. Having a friendly, professional-looking headshot on your site works a lot better than some random selfie you posted on Instagram.
- **A few lines speaking to potential readers who stumble across your blog and want to know what you're about.** This lets me know the type of audience you are trying to attract. This might say, "Hey guys! Welcome to my blog. If you want Carrie Bradshaw's closet, but you're super broke, this is the site for you. We'll talk about how to look high fashion on a low budget and how to find the best sales and deals the Internet has to offer." From this I would gather your audience is on the younger side, loves *Sex and the City* and Manhattan, and wants to be stylish on a super lean budget. That means I probably wouldn't pick you for a crazy expensive purse, but I would choose you for a semi-annual sale for a major department store.

- **One video from your YouTube page, most likely your trailer.** This lets me see how you are on camera without clicking out to your YouTube profile. If you don't have a trailer, pick your favorite video that gives a real sense of your personality. And if you're still working on your YouTube presence, just upload a video of yourself saying your name, what your site is about, and where we can follow you to see more of your content. Make it look nice, but it doesn't have to be super edited. It's just to help me hear your voice and see your personality. @thegreylayers is a perfect example of why this is necessary. Her photos are very editorial with an elevated attitude, but when I met her she was super bubbly and down to earth. Talk about versatility! It completely opened up the possibilities for her, because I knew if it was a video campaign we could do all sorts of fun beauty tutorials and she would still be a good fit.

- **Three to five of your favorite Instagram posts.** This lets me check out what *you* think are your best pieces of content. Make sure to embed these, just like you embedded your YouTube trailer; I don't want to have to click through to get to your Instagram page. Highlight your range and include posts from different categories and different styles: style, beauty, travel, flat lay, etc.

Now I know the persona you're presenting to your audience and can determine, at least on the surface, what type of person is following you. The next page you want to spend a lot of time on is your partnership/collaboration page.

PARTNERSHIP PAGE

Some of the content on your partnership page will be a repeat of what's on your about page. And that's okay, because you never know which page a casting director will land on. She may go straight to the partnership page to see if you're game for her campaign before she researches you some more. Don't make her have to read through your partnership page and then *have to* read your about page. It should all be in one spot and read pretty much like a cover letter/résumé:

- **Different hi-res photo of your face.** See previously.

- **Name, what you do, and three things that describe you.** *XYZ influencer is a style blogger who loves dogs, wine, and affordable clothing.*

- **Where are you from and where do you live.** *A native of Miami, Florida, XYZ went to Rutgers University in New Jersey, Go Knights!, and after graduating with a BA in economics moved to New York City. After a few too many cold winters, she headed west and now calls Los Angeles home.*

- **What you do/did for work.** *XYZ worked for a few fashion brands in the finance department, but she was always more interested in patterns and fabrics than Excel spreadsheets and pie graphs. In 2015, she took the plunge to work on her blog full-time and she hasn't looked back since.*

- **Things we might not know about you**. *In her spare time XYZ loves looking for gems at flea markets and on eBay and has never met an estate sale she didn't like. She also takes karate, jujitsu, and Krav Maga three times each week. She's not very good, but she feels like a badass after each class. When she's not shopping or exercising, she's working with XYZ charities to provide women who are looking to get back on their feet with chic clothing for job interviews.*

- **Anything else.** *You'll usually find XYZ hanging with her boyfriend Chris, her best friend Meredith, or her dog Roxy.*

Now I don't know about you, but this is the greatest biography I have never seen. I know her name, her three favorite things, where she's lived and where she lives now, where she went to school, what she did for a living, that she's super into shopping and exercising, she does charity work, and that she has a boyfriend, a best friend, and a dog. I've just thought of seven campaigns XYZ would be perfect for and she doesn't even exist. Is she perfect? Well yes, because she is fictional, but you should strive to be as well-rounded as she is.

On your partnership page you should also list the types of collaborations and projects you are interested in doing/have done. It might look something like this:

XYZ influencer is available for collaboration on the following projects:

- *Ambassadorships*
- *Sponsored blogs, vlogs, and social posts*
- *Facebook Live videos*
- *Events and meet and greets*
- *Photo and video shoots*
- *Other projects that will help tell your story to my engaged audience*

All content created will be promoted with at least one Instagram Story, single post, or gallery. Rates will vary depending on scope of work, usage, and exclusivity, but please reach out to me with all budget levels. I would love to learn more about your objectives and figure out ways we can work together within your budget. Contact me at firstname@nameofblog.com.

This is NOT the place to put giant logos from all the brands you've done campaigns with because one of their competitors might see that and not hire you. We learned this lesson in Chapter 2 and it applies here as well. What you CAN do is create a category for all of your sponsored posts and link to them. That way, if brands want to do the extra legwork they can, but you won't unnecessarily take yourself out of the running.

CONTACT PAGE

If you have a really robust partnership page, you won't really need much on your contact page. It can be really simple like:

If you are a brand and you'd like to collaborate, please email firstname@nameofblog.com.

If you are a publicist, a member of the press, or a reader of the blog and you'd like to get in touch, please email info@nameofblog.com.

You can pretty much use any variation of this and it will work. One thing you should not do is have a contact form and nothing else. I usually put a lot of time and effort into my outreach letters and oftentimes want to send an attachment so influencers can have a better sense of what I'm describing. When I see a contact form it makes me want to give up because all my beautiful formatting gets lost and I can't attach anything. And if for some reason you don't respond and I want to follow up, I'll need to fill out the form again. Why are you making it so hard for me to give you money?

The only thing worse than a contact form is having no contact information at all. There have been numerous times when I've looked on an influencer's blog for her contact information and not found it. Or I found an email and it bounced back. Help me help you!

Now that your digital house is in order, it's time to get on people's radars.

BLOGGER ROUNDUPS

I'm sure you've seen these roundups on the internet: "10 Design Instagrams You Must Follow" or "The 25 Most Stylish Bloggers In New York" or "12 YouTubers To Follow If You Want To See English and Spanish Language Videos." You may think it's difficult to get on those lists, but it's really not. All you need to do is head on over to the website and find one of these roundups. Look up the person who wrote it and get in contact with them. If they have an email you can shoot them a note that says something like:

> *Hi Writer,*
>
> *I wanted to thank you for compiling the roundup on [insert roundup where you found them]. I really like XYZ influencer you included and started following her for inspiration.*
>
> *My name is XYZ and I am a [beauty, fashion, travel, lifestyle, fitness, etc.] blogger/vlogger from XYZ city. I recently hit [25K/50k/100K] followers and wanted to send you a note in case you are working on future roundups where I might be a fit. I'd be more than happy to send you my press kit or my one-sheet if you'd like more information. You can also check out my blog, YouTube, and Instagram.*
>
> *Thank you so much for your time,*
> *Influencer*

Now I can't guarantee you that you'll end up in a future roundup, but if this doesn't give you a fighting chance, nothing will. If you can't find an email address for the person, feel free to follow her on Instagram. If it feels right in your bones, tweak this message a bit and slide into her DMs. It sounds a little stalker-ish, but if you're polite and your content is good, she shouldn't mind. People do it to me all the time, and I either follow them back or add them to my database so I don't forget about them.

One way to definitely be included in a blogger roundup is to create your own. It sounds crazy, but there are quite a few people I have found because they used this tactic. There's no shame in creating a blog post called "10 Style Bloggers from Houston You Should Be Following" finding nine other accounts you think people should be following, and writing a little blurb on each one with some photos and links. You'll make some friends in the process and when I google "style bloggers from Houston" your site will probably come up. One word of advice: Make yourself the first blogger. I know some bloggers think they shouldn't do this because it will make them seem full of themselves, but sometimes I find who I need before I get to the end of the list or my search gets cut short. How sad would it be if you put yourself all the way at the bottom and I never got to you?

PR MAILING LISTS

Long before influencers were getting paid crazy amounts to create content, they would create content in exchange for free products, services, and VIP access. Since pretty much everyone and their mom now demands a fee before they post anywhere, you can become a publicist's new BFF by posting for free . . . for now.

Most publicists work on retainer and as part of their job they need to secure placements for their clients. Of course they want to be in all the big newspapers, magazines, and websites, but smaller businesses would be super happy appearing on your site as well. If your audience is in their target demo and your content looks nice, you should have yourself a partnership.

I'm sure you are bombarded with ads for new products and services on Facebook and Instagram. Well, these brands are potential partners for you. If you see a brand you like, head over to its website and look for the "press" link; it's usually at the bottom. On that page you'll find press releases, hi-res images, and ta-da, an email for its publicist. You can send her a note that looks like this:

> *Dear Publicist,*
>
> *My name is XYZ and I am the blogger behind nameofblog.com and @instagramhandle.*
>
> *I recently saw an ad for XYZ product on Facebook, and after doing some research, I realized this is totally something I would buy for XYZ reason.*
>
> *I recently hit [25K/50k/100K] followers and XK page views per month and wanted to reach out and discuss a*

possible partnership. In exchange for complimentary product, I would write a 250- to 500-word post about your product complete with custom photos and will promote the blog post on my Instagram channel. I think this product would be a great addition to my makeup bag and a product my audience would love to know about.

If possible, I would also love to get a quote from the founder to give my post that personal touch. If this is something you would be interested in, I'd be more than happy to send you my press kit or my one-sheet. If you'd like more information about me you can check out my blog, YouTube, and Instagram.

Thank you so much for your time,
Influencer

What a great note, and not just because I wrote it, but because it covers all the bases:

1. **You've introduced yourself, told them how you found them, and why you like their product.** By the way, it's important to not use this technique to load up on free stuff that you don't actually like. Publicists hate that, and your audience

will hate that. You've read Part 1 of this book so you should know better, but I just HAD to state it here to make sure I am covering my bases.

2. **You've let them know your stats and what you're offering.** This shows them you understand partnerships are a two-way street and you're bringing something to the table. You're also showing them that you're honest, but hopeful, and are asking for a quote that will personalize the post so that it really resonates with your audience.

3. **You've pointed them to your work and opened the door for a follow-up.** By letting them know you're happy to follow up with more information, you're putting the ball in their court and allowing them to check you out before responding.

If you don't hear from them in a week, you can send a follow-up note. If you still don't hear back, it's their loss, and you can move on to someone who would love to work with you!

BRANDS AND CASTING AGENTS

Once you've been featured in a roundup or two and have a few PR partnerships under your belt, it's time for the big leagues: approaching brands and casting agents directly. It may seem like a big task to take on, but again, if you have great content and approach them in a mindful way, they'll be happy to hear from you.

Before you can send them an email, you'll need to make sure you have the right contact, and LinkedIn is your go-to for that. You should search for people who have a title that has the word "influencer" or "talent partnerships" in it. Be sure to read their descriptions so you're not contacting anyone in HR, as that's a different type of talent. Another way to find the key players is to comb through sites like digiday.com and adage.com and see who they're quoting in their articles about influencers. These are usually the people you want to get in touch with. If you can't find an email address for the person who handles influencer marketing, sometimes a quick message on Facebook or Instagram to the brand's handle will do the trick. I actually booked a decor blogger and gave her a home makeover because she sent the brand a Facebook message. We just so happened to be looking for a blogger in her area when she messaged us. She scored free services AND cash because she wasn't afraid to reach out and connect.

Once you've found them, you want to send a message that's a mix between the media and the PR notes mentioned previously. It should look like the following:

> *Dear Casting Director,*
>
> *My name is XYZ and I am a [style, beauty, fitness, travel, lifestyle, etc.] blogger from XYZ city. I recently hit [25K/50K/100K] followers and wanted to send you a note in case you are working on future campaigns where I might be a fit.*
>
> *I am a big fan of your [product/ service/website] for XYZ reason and believe my readers would really enjoy a collaboration with your brand.*
>
> *If this is something you might be interested in, I'd be more than happy to send you my press kit or my one-sheet. If you'd like more information about me you can check out my blog, YouTube, and Instagram.*
>
> *Thank you so much for your time,*
> *Influencer*

Short, sweet, and to the point. These emails are great to send directly to brands because they love collaborating with people who organically use their product. I love getting these kinds of emails because they help me connect with people I might have never found. Every campaign is so different that it might take months for me to find something they're right for, but they're on my radar, so mission accomplished.

WHAT IS A PRESS KIT AND WHAT IS A ONE-SHEET?

Oh, did you think I was going to leave you hanging? Of course not. A press kit is really just your "about," "partnerships," and "contact" pages rolled up into a nice pdf. I save every press kit I'm sent because I can search them for keywords like "musician" and "vegan." As I am writing this, I received a request for an influencer who has recently switched to a plant-based diet. The girl who has that in her press kit . . . hired. Your one-sheet is all the crucial elements from your press kit on—you got it—one sheet.

If you do not have fantastic design skills, I suggest hiring someone to create these documents for you. The last thing you want to do is finally convince someone to request your press kit or your one-sheet only to turn them off because you sent them an ugly document. Oh, and never, ever, ever put prices in your press kit. Why would you limit yourself in a document so permanent? Don't do it.

These tips should help you package your brand, but at the end of the day, creating a brand as an influencer is very similar to creating a brand as an employee. And rule number one in the workplace and in life is: BE NICE. Almost anything can be forgiven if you are nice. More money magically appears for influencers who are nice. Being nice is also more important than how many followers you have. It always has been, and it always will be.

INFLUENCER INSIGHT

The best piece of advice I can give is the one I received a long time ago when I was just starting on my path in the United States: "Say a little, do a lot, be kind." For content creation, this formula translates into:

- **Don't blab about your plans and ideas, or someone else will implement them before you do.** The influencer market is a competitive place today. I wish I didn't have to learn that principle the hard way.
- **Be prepared to work your *** off at any time, but for the first couple of years also be prepared to not get paid much for it,**

just yet. Treat the work that you may not be getting paid for as IF you were getting top dollar for it. After all, the content you create is your reputation.

- **Be kind. Always.** Sometimes people you have to work with are simply . . . not very nice. I'd like to use a different word here, but let's keep it G-rated. But keep your cool. Vent to someone who you trust, but smile and just smooth the situations over. This is essential in any business, but in influencer marketing it's everything.

As far as content creation goes, one of my biggest regrets up to this date is that I didn't go with my gut and instead listened too much to advice that was freely given on how to succeed. Read it all, but use your head and trust your gut in the end.

Don't be afraid to hire help! Share your pay if you are running low on creative ideas. It's well worth it in the end!

—@livingnotes

INFLUENCER ICON

JOY CHO

@ohjoy + ohjoy.com

If you find yourself talking about influencers who have built empires, Joy's name will definitely be mentioned. An early adopter of Pinterest, where she has over twelve million followers, she has multiple lines at Target, and has authored three books. She built her brand from scratch, now has several employees, and everyone in the DIY space knows her name. Have you seen some of her work? Not even on my best day am I churning out sliders that look like that!

ON PINTEREST VS. INSTAGRAM . . .

Pinterest is my dominant platform as far as the number of followers, but you have to look at every platform differently, as it's not all about numbers. Engagement is super important, too. I was one of the early users on Pinterest, and my blog audience instantly followed me there. I also had a lot of great online write-ups where people were listing me as someone to follow on Pinterest. So it grew really fast. I still love Pinterest and use it every day as a tool for my business and to amplify my blog content. Lately, Instagram has also become a go-to platform for sharing and connecting with my audience. There is such a great community there, where followers can reach out through messaging and comments and really connect with me and the Oh Joy brand.

ON PRODUCING HIGH-QUALITY CONTENT . . .

Creating content should be about sharing ideas that you really love and feel genuine to you. It can be easy to look at what other successful brands or bloggers are doing and emulate their photos or content on your platform, but focus on what makes you YOU. And what you can create that feels different and feels special to your voice and your story.

There's not a huge difference between "organic" and "branded" content for me. Everything appearing on my platforms is in line with my aesthetic of bright colors, touches of whimsy, and above all, hopefully bringing joy to people's lives. Yes, when you work with a brand, there are certain requirements from the brand you need to adhere to, but you also need to find out what those things are up front and make sure you can still tell a story in your voice with those requirements. If you can't, then kindly pass on the opportunity.

ON WORKING FOR FREE . . .

I would definitely recommend working for free (or for exposure) if you are just starting your brand or platform, and still trying to build an audience or opportunities. We all have to start somewhere. I did a lot of free (or cheap) work when I was starting my business and trying to grow my portfolio to show people what I could do. Once you build up momentum, you can be more selective and be firm in your fees.

ON ASSUMING YOU'LL HAVE MORE TIME FOR YOUR CHILDREN WHEN YOU OWN YOUR OWN BUSINESS . . .

The ironic thing about that assumption is that starting your own business (and maintaining it) requires more time than a nine-to-five day job. Yes, you can have more flexibility because you are in control of your hours, but it's not something to go into thinking you will have more time. The time is just dispersed differently.

"Working from home" while taking care of kids is near impossible when you are actually trying to do it. All the moms that I know who run businesses are working well into the night many nights a week. I have the ability to end my workday before 4 P.M. so I can pick my kids up from school, but that also means that I am working again for a few hours most nights after they go to bed. Yes, you can take vacations without asking your "boss," but on vacations you are likely checking emails and doing some sort of business maintenance since it's hard to completely shut yourself off from work when you run your own business.

If I had started my business after becoming a mom, I would have been better about saying no to things that weren't worth my time or money earlier than I did in actuality. Once you become a parent, your time is so much more valuable because you weigh whether something is worth doing and being away from your kids for. That ability has helped me a lot in business as well.

ON HAVING YOUR CHILDREN APPEAR IN YOUR ONLINE WORK . . .

You do sometimes see my family on social media, but it has changed a lot for me over the years. When my blog was my only online outlet and when the Oh Joy community was much smaller, my blog felt a bit more personal and I shared a lot of everyday family moments that my readers could connect with. But as my kids got older, I have chosen to show them less and less. You will see them pop up on my IG and IG stories every so often, but they are rarely on the blog.

For me, the personal moments I share are meant to add a bit of joy, inspiration, tips, or ideas that people can relate to or help them personally in some way. The inclusion of my kids (or not) will continue to evolve as they get older. More than anything, I make sure whatever I share is what is comfortable for me and my family. Every family or situation is different, and there is no one right way. You have to do what makes sense for you. If you do choose to show your kids on social media, a few things I suggest:

- Never show the outside of your home or your children's school.

- Don't discuss when you are home alone or your partner is out of town.
- Don't post your location or what you are doing in real time. You can save it all and post later.
- Respect your kids and their moments. Never force them to take a photo for social media. If they are old enough, ask for their permission too.

ON FINANCING YOUR PASSIONS . . .

My entire business has been built on my own money. No investors, no borrowing money from family, etc. Because I started my business as a freelance designer, there was no up-front investment; I already had a computer and printer, which is all I really needed. I built up my clients and work, but really was mostly making what I needed to pay my bills. So when I decided to start a stationery line back in 2007, I didn't have any extra money just sitting there in a savings account. I used my credit card to fund the production of my first stationery collection. After that, I used what I made from it to put back into the next collection. It wasn't ideal to rack up credit card debt, but it was the only way I would have been able to do it at that time.

While I recommend having money saved before you start your business, if you can, I also wouldn't change what I did because it would have taken me years to save up enough to get started, and the timing and results would have been much different. I only continued that stationery line for a few years because it was draining my resources financially and I didn't like living like that. Currently, any products we create are through a license, so there is no up-front cost on my end for production, and it allows me to focus on the more fun aspects of designing products.

ON HIRING A TEAM . . .

My business started in 2005 as me working by myself from home. I had an intern in the first few years, then I worked with some outside freelancers for a few years. But it wasn't until 2014 that I hired my first employees to work side by side with me at an office outside of my home. It took me eight years to feel comfortable taking the leap and the financial risk to hire. I started small, with one part-time employee, then added another, then another, and then those part-time folks came on full-time within a year. Then, I added one or two new team members every year after that. Everyone has their own specific role, from designing to styling to crafting to social media to new business. I work directly with all of them in some way every day and oversee the business and creative direction of Oh Joy!

ON TAKING IT TO THE NEXT LEVEL . . .

In 2004, after seeing a girl at Target covet some pj's I designed as part of my then job as a designer for Cynthia Rowley's Swell line, I made it a goal to one day have my own line at Target. I didn't necessarily know how to reach that goal, but my focus on growing my business and portfolio was to work toward that. Of course, you never know what will pan out in real life. But ten years later, that dream came to fruition with our first collection at Target in 2014.

While not every single thing you put on your goal list works out, I sincerely believe that if you want something badly enough, and work hard at it, you can manifest your goals. Everything you do—all your work, everything you learn—is in preparation to reach that goal. In the earlier days of my business, I reached out to brands like Anthropologie and Urban Outfitters to do design work for them, and built up my portfolio with work that represented my style and showed people what I could do.

My biggest advice for anyone with a similar goal is to keep putting yourself out there and show work that you want to be making (even if no one is hiring you to do that work yet). I think the biggest misconception is that these things fell into my lap, and that's not true. Ninety percent of the bigger projects I've worked on were from me reaching out and pitching my work and ideas to a brand.

ON WOMEN DOMINATING INFLUENCER MARKETING . . .

I love that women are owning the social media space and have the ability to create content and earn a living off of it. We all have a story and a voice, and we live in a time where we have platforms to share our voice with the world if we want to.

No one actually lives an "Insta-ready" life. I think the idea that anyone does is an assumption we all need to get rid of. If your business is based in social media, you are certainly thinking about capturing things in a different way than someone who doesn't use social media. But we all have to keep in mind that what we share on social media is such a small fragment of our lives.

I think most people who share regularly on social media are very aware of turning that switch off and on when it makes sense for them. This is why I love things like Instagram Stories that give a bit more of an authentic window into people's days. It's less perfect, less edited, and people can connect with you beyond the perfect pretty picture.

My advice for young women who want to create content:

- **Do your research.** Since there are so many bloggers and influencers these days, it's important to make sure you're doing something that's different and not too similar to what's already out there (both in subject matter and aesthetic). You might see someone else achieving success with a certain style or voice, but instead of imitating them, use it to fuel the fire of your goals to grow in your own way.
- **Be genuine.** Post about the things that you really love and would be excited to share every day.

- **Don't stress.** It can be easy to worry about getting readers or trying to grow an audience or the "numbers." But if you are creative, authentic, and are doing something different, people will tune in.

ON HINDSIGHT BEING 20/20 . . .

The journey, the trials, the hardships—those make the experience sweeter and the reward greater. I don't know that I would change anything about the beginning or avoid some of the tough times, because they made me into the woman and wife and mother and business owner that I am. Experience (good and bad) is necessary for success, so I don't want to shy away from that.

While social media is definitely essential to the success of a business these days, the most important thing? YOU BE YOU. Because social media allows us to see so much (maybe sometimes too much) of what everyone else is doing, it also makes us compare ourselves to others more than ever. So stick to who you are—your style, your voice, and what you believe in.

PART 3

Monetizing Your Influence

CHAPTER 5

The Money

How do you determine and negotiate your worth?

Congratulations! After creating amazing content and getting your name out there, someone has discovered you and wants to collaborate on a campaign. They pop on over to your Instagram, quickly find your email address (thanks, Chapter 2) and shoot over a soft offer to see if you're interested, available, and within budget. The ones I send read something like this:

> *Hi Influencer,*
>
> *I have a great opportunity for you. I'm working on XYZ campaign and we would love to fly you to New York on ABC date.*
>
> *We're looking for you to do a one-day shoot and post one Instagram post. For this scope we have a budget of $$$$. Let*

me know if this is something you'd be interested in and if you're available.

Thanks,
Casting Agent

Now, this might seem like Life Lessons 101, but when someone sends you an email, the polite thing to do is to send one back. Unless it's a chain email, then feel free to send that straight to the trash because absolutely no one has time for that. But you would be shocked, SHOCKED I tell you, at the number of emails I have sent that remain unanswered. Emails that have MONEY in them. Real, actual, US of A dollars. Not the promise of money from some foreign prince who will wire it over after you text him your Social Security number.

EXPERT TIP

The most common mistake influencers make that could easily be avoided is not answering their emails.

—Beca Alexander (@becaalexander), president and founder at Socialyte

I don't know about you, but I am certainly not in a position to turn down $5,000 for eight hours of work and one Instagram post. And yet, this happens all the time. Did the $5,000 shock you? Now make that number $25,000. Make it $50,000. Hell, let's get crazy and make it $100,000. These girls have more money sitting in their inboxes than some people will see all year and yet here they are, too busy arranging croissants on a plate to answer a simple email.

Even if you're traveling or otherwise unavailable, there is no excuse for not responding. This is the age of modern technology. You don't have to yell your food order into a phone, hail a taxi, or stand in line to buy groceries. You can do all these things with an app. So, I find it a little hard to believe that these girls can't just turn on an out-of-office message that says, "Hi there. Thanks for emailing. I'm traveling at the moment but will respond to your message as soon as I can. If this is a time-sensitive opportunity, please forward your email to urgent@nameofblog.com or call/text me at 555.555.5555."

So simple, and yet . . .

DON'T BE THAT GIRL

Every time I send an offer letter and the influencer doesn't respond, it always makes me a little sad, and not because she is missing a great opportunity. I mean she definitely is, but this is business and the show must go on. My heart breaks a little because without fail, each and every time, she'll write back three days too late freaking out and asking me if the opportunity is still available. I really want to send her a meme of Scrooge McDuck diving into a pile of money that says, "This Could Be You, but You Playin'," but I'm a nice person, so I just reply to her panicked email with the following:

> *Hey there!*
>
> *Thank you so much for getting back to me. Unfortunately, we've already selected an influencer for this campaign, but we'll definitely keep you in mind for future opportunities.*
>
> *Brittany*

Now if we're being completely honest, which we are, I'm probably never going to pitch her again. Sometimes I need to find and secure an influencer in 48 hours, and I absolutely do not have time for people who take days to respond to an email. All it tells me is that this is a hobby for them. If I wanted to find hobbyists, I could go to an arts and crafts store. We are here to work, people.

Okay, so you get an email offering you a campaign, and you're totally going to answer it because I just explained what happens if you don't, and it has a specific budget in it. How do you know if it's fair or not? It's time to talk money. You need to learn what your work is worth and how much you should charge. This is actually one of the most difficult parts of being an influencer. Ask for a fee that's too high and you'll risk pricing yourself out. Too low and you'll undersell yourself and people might doubt your worth. Either way you may come off as someone who is new to the game and easy to take advantage of. If you can command high fees because your content is that professional, great, but be realistic and have patience. It may take you a while to find your sweet spot, but once you do, you'll be on your way to becoming a full-time influencer.

THE FIVE FEE FACTORS

Since you're following the 70/30 rule from Chapter 2, you have limited space for branded content, but if you decide to take on a particular sponsored project, you need to figure out what your involvement should be worth to the brand.

Now you might say, "Brittany, if my favorite brand wanted to work with me I would do it for free. I might even offer to pay them." If you're so ecstatic about a campaign that you would participate even if they weren't paying you, that's great! But it costs money to create great branded content, so you're going to need a budget to work with.

You might also say, "Brittany, I don't like talking about money." And you would not be alone. Most people, women in particular, are intimidated by negotiations. That's why it is so important to figure out how much you are worth and be confident in that number. It will help you stay strong when negotiating and help you realize when a campaign is not worth the time/effort and you should just walk away. There may be times when you might lower your fee because you want to meet the brand in the middle, but remember, clothing, trips, and beauty products cannot pay your rent or your student loans.

Negotiating is less frightening once you've figured out the numbers. Whether it's a blog post, Instagram post, or YouTube video, the formula for what to charge is simple:

Distribution Fee + Talent Fee = What You Should Charge

Let's start by understanding the difference between your distribution fee and your talent fee.

Your *distribution fee* is how much it costs to be featured on your channel/blog. Keep in mind this price can vary greatly based on five factors:

1. **Follower Count.** This is simply how many followers you have.

2. **Engagement.** Of all your followers, what percentage of people liked/commented on your content in the past month? How do you know you've made it? When your engagement on branded content posts is as high, or even higher, than your organic content. If this is true for you, like it is for @effortlyss, shout it from the hilltops. This tells me you are making wise decisions with the money brands give you, investing in production quality (e.g., renting a unique space for the backdrop, hiring a professional videographer, etc.) to make sure the content performs. These are the sorts of things that make me happy, and when I am happy I give you more money!

3. **Quality of Content.** If brands are contacting you, your content is good, but how good is it? I've worked on campaigns where the content was so good, it was dropped right onto a billboard, into a magazine, or turned into a television commercial. This is your goal, not only because it solidifies your status as a true

content creator, but also because that kind of usage is premium and you can make more money!

4. **Name/Facial Recognition/Skills.** More often than not, brands will share your content on their social channels, and it's usually received very well by their audience. But if the influencer has a recognizable name/face, when the brands share, the comments turn from "great shot" to "OMG I LOOOOOVE XYZ INFLUENCER." That's a win for them and a BIG win for you. Similarly, if you're an amazing dancer, or make the best-looking cakes, they're also paying for access to your skills—which you have probably spent years honing—to make this piece of content really stand out. Skills = Time, and Time = Money.

5. **Demographics.** This is when it definitely pays to have a niche. If a brand is looking for college students who live in a particular city and would die to have their new eye palette, and that's your audience, you're instantly much more valuable to a brand than another influencer who only speaks to one of those target demos.

Your *talent fee* is how much it actually costs you to create the content. This number includes all costs associated with the campaign and your hourly rate. To figure out a basic minimum budget, calculate the cost of:

- Your photographer/photo editor
- The space where you'll be shooting (hotel room, Airbnb, etc.)
- Any props you'll need to purchase (food, candles, flowers, balloons)
- Any clothing you'll need to buy (Sometimes a campaign will cause you to shoot off-season—a winter fashion spread in the summer—and you'll need to buy new clothes so the content looks fresh when you post it months later.)

Then you need to factor in your hourly rate. Whether you're writing a blog post, self-producing a photo/video shoot, or working on set, those things take time and time is money. If you're just beginning, you might start at $25 an hour and increase your hourly rate as you have more experience and campaigns under your belt. Activities under this hourly rate will differ depending on the campaign, but should include:

- Negotiating with the casting agent (1 hour)
- Reading the brief and researching the advertiser (2 hours)
- Scouting and securing a location (2 hours)
- Creating a mood board of the shoot (2 hours)
- Shooting the content (up to 10 hours)

You add these two together, and that is how much you should charge. You can take a look at this handy, dandy chart that will provide you with a healthy range for each tier.

	Distribution Fee		**Talent Fee**
Follower and/or Subscriber Count	**Instagram Post**	**YouTube Video**	**Photo and/or Video Shoot**
10K–99K	$250–$2,000	$1,000–$5,000	$500–$2,000
100K–499K	$2,000–$5,000	$5,000–$10,000	$2,000–$7,000
500K–999K	$5,000–$10,000	$10,000–$25,000	$7,000–$15,000
1MM+	$7,500+	$15,000+	$10,000+

NEGOTIATING YOUR COMPENSATION

Let's say you have 100,000 followers (look at you!) and the brand wants you to do a one-day shoot and an Instagram post. You could ask for $4,000 and it would be within reason. Now, within reason doesn't mean that's the minimum or the maximum, because, like I said, your actual fee will change depending on the five fee factors, but it means no one will roll their eyes at you for requesting that amount of money. And really, in this game, keeping people from rolling their eyes at you is half the battle.

If the letter you received from the casting agent is close to what you think you're worth, then go ahead and let them know you'd like to receive more details. Your email should look something like this:

> *Hi Casting Agent,*
>
> *Thank you so much for thinking of me for XYZ campaign. I am free on that date, and that budget is in line with my fee for a one-day shoot and one Instagram post.*
>
> *Would you be able to send along full details or a contract for review? I would love to see the terms and usage before formally accepting.*
>
> *Thank you,*
> *Influencer*

But what do you do if the original email offered you free products or services in exchange for your work? Well, then you need to ask yourself a few important questions.

IS THIS FOR A CAMPAIGN OR FOR COVERAGE?

When a brand asks you to include certain talking points/hashtags in your post and have a time frame for when they want the coverage to go live, it's considered branded content or a campaign. But not every email you receive will be for branded content. Publicists reach out to influencers all the time with the hope that you'll like their client's product/service and will share it with your followers. They're just looking for coverage. If the email you receive doesn't make it clear what they're actually looking for, google the person who sent it to you. Check out the person's website or LinkedIn. Does the person work for the company whose products you were sent, an agency, a publisher, or a public relations firm? If they sent a press release, you can safely assume they're a publicist looking for coverage. But if all else fails, just ask. Both publicists and casting directors have a desired outcome, and they won't be shy about letting you know what that is.

If the email is from a publicist, and they're looking for coverage in exchange for products/services, you can decide if you'd like to do it or not. If it's for a campaign, then you have to ask yourself the next question.

WHAT'S IN IT FOR ME?

Will doing this campaign for free be worth it? You can break that question down into three parts:

1. **Is it for your dream company?** Maybe you've always wanted to work with this specific company, especially if it's a luxury brand, and this is your first chance.

2. **Will you get to travel?** Maybe they will send you on an amazing trip where you can kick your content up a notch.

3. **Are they going to promote you?** Maybe they aren't willing to pay you, but they will do a profile on their site and share your content with their community.

These are all good reasons to say yes to an unpaid campaign. But if you answered "no" to these three questions, you should probably turn down the gig. Any time you spend on this campaign will be time you aren't spending on your organic content, the content that will lead you to paid work. You also risk putting a brand on your channels that will alienate competitors and keep them from hiring you. Unless it's worth it, don't risk it. You can send them an email that looks like this:

Hi Casting Agent,

Thank you so much for thinking of me for XYZ campaign. This sounds like a great opportunity because [XYZ brand is one of my favorites/I'm excited to travel on behalf of XYZ brand/I'm excited to be introduced to the XYZ community].

Since there is no monetary compensation, would XYZ brand be able to feature me on their site and/or share my content on their social channels? [Only include this part if they're not offering it.]

Would you be able to send along full details or a contract for review? I would love to see the terms and usage before formally accepting.

Thank you,
Influencer

What if they offered you money but it's less than you think you're worth? First things first, check your ego. If your friend came to you with the same opportunity, would you tell her to go for it, or to hold out for more money? We're usually more honest with our friends than we are with ourselves, so this is a great viewpoint to take. If you've concluded that it's unfair, you should send the following email:

Hi Casting Agent,

Thank you so much for thinking of me for XYZ campaign. This sounds like a great opportunity because XYZ brand is one of my favorites.

For the scope you requested in your email, my rate is closer to [$$$$]. Is this something you would be able to accommodate?

If so, would you be able to send along full details or a contract for review? I would love to see the terms and usage before formally accepting.

Thank you,
Influencer

This is what is called a counteroffer and puts the ball back in the casting agent's court. Countering makes a lot of people nervous, but it shouldn't if you are countering with a fair price and aren't doing it to be greedy. One of two things will happen: They will accept your counteroffer and send over a contract, or they will deny your counteroffer and ask if you still want to participate. If they deny you, revisit the three questions under "What's in it for me?" and make your decision. If you decide to go for it, send the below:

Hi Casting Agent,

I'm excited to be on board for this campaign. In addition to [$$$$ compensation], would XYZ brand be able to feature me on their site and/or share my content on their social channels? [Only include this part if they're not offering it.]

I'll stand by for the official offer/contract.

Thank you,
Influencer

PASSING ON AN OPPORTUNITY

Sometimes the financial stars do not align, and it's just not worth it for you to participate in a campaign. This is a problem that happens more and more as you gain followers and popularity and do more campaigns. You see, with each campaign, you're aligning yourself with a brand and promising you won't work with any of their competitors no matter what they're offering. You're essentially cutting off future revenue streams. So, you need to choose each campaign wisely, and it needs to be worth it.

If you decide to pass, you absolutely must pass with grace or you will be banned and never work in this town again. Okay, that sounds a bit dramatic, but it's 100 percent true. Ask anyone was has ever worked with me. I keep a running list of influencers who are terrible to work with and will share it with anyone who asks. It's not that hard to pass politely, so I don't know why so many people are terrible at doing it.

If they wanted you to participate for free:

> *Hi Casting Agent,*
>
> *Thank you so much for thinking of me for XYZ campaign. I really appreciate it, but I am not participating in unpaid campaigns at this time.*
>
> *If there is an increase in your budget, I would be more than happy to revisit this campaign.*
>
> *Thank you,*
> *Influencer*

If they wanted you to participate for less than you were willing:

> *Hi Casting Agent,*
>
> *Thank you so much for thinking of me for XYZ campaign. I really appreciate it, but I do not think I can deliver the high-quality branded content this campaign deserves with the compensation offered.*

If there is an increase in your budget, I would be more than happy to revisit this campaign.

Thank you,
Influencer

It's 100 percent okay to pass because an advertiser doesn't have the budget to pay what you think you're worth. It happens all the time when people apply for jobs, so it shouldn't be any different here. Sometimes, a casting agent was playing hardball with you and will accept your counteroffer after you've passed. Other times, if they really want you, they will reallocate money from another part of the budget to give it to you. You never really know what's happening on the other end of the email, which is why it's crucial to be firm but polite.

What should you do if you're passing because the campaign was not on brand for you? Unfortunately, this happens because many companies are still new to influencer marketing and have not yet figured out which influencers are on brand or how to approach them. But since you don't want to work on the campaign, this is the easiest email to write:

Hi Casting Agent,

Thank you so much for thinking of me for XYZ campaign. I know that engagements are probably an important metric for you, but I don't think the

> *content I would create for this campaign will resonate with my audience. I want to make sure you have a great return on your investment, so I will need to decline your offer. However, please feel free to reach out again with your next campaign.*
>
> *Thank you,*
> *Influencer*

But if you're lucky, every campaign you're offered will be on brand and either be in line with your fee, or will have enough bells and whistles to make it worth it. Then you're off to the toughest, but last stop before you can begin a campaign: finalizing a contract and deciphering the brief.

EXPERT TIP

A big mistake influencers make is following the paychecks as opposed to road-mapping a list of brands that they are passionate about. It is crucial to build long-lasting relationships with brand partners that feel authentic to your fans and their consumers.

—Maximilian Ulanoff (@maximilian_ulanoff), talent agent at Buchwald

INFLUENCER ICON

TENI PANOSIAN

@tenipanosian + remarques.com

If you follow beauty influencers on Instagram or YouTube, there is a very good chance you know who Teni is. She has partnered with the biggest and best names in makeup, skincare, and fashion. She created a Halloween makeup tutorial for a pharaoh look a few years ago and it is still one of my favorite YouTube videos of all time. She's also one of the few bloggers who has been really open with her personal and professional growth over the last few years. And she has a master's of communication management from USC. Yeah, she's definitely more than just a pretty face.

ON CHANGING THE NAME OF YOUR BLOG FROM MISSMAVEN TO REMARQUES . . .

I knew it was time for a change because I hadn't been feeling inspired to produce blog content for some time—about a year. I did some reflecting and discovered I'd outgrown the name, and that sparked a fresh eagerness: I had an opportunity to start a completely new blog.

I knew I wanted the personality of this new blog to be elevated and altogether more mature than MissMaven.com, which had started to feel juvenile. I wanted to keep the name easy and uncomplicated, so I decided this new site would simply be my remarks on different aspects of my life. This was a particularly big step for me, because my blog was how I entered the digital world in the first place. It had become so embedded in my professional identity that, certainly, I was very nervous to find out how my audience would receive the change. Thankfully, as people who grow and change themselves, they were very supportive, and I couldn't have been more thrilled about that!

ON THE YOUTUBE STRATEGY THAT HELPED YOU HIT 1,000,000 SUBSCRIBERS . . .

The strategy has always been to create quality content, consistently. People want to see that you're serious about maintaining a content channel, so they'll keep coming back, in the same way that they know their favorite television show is on prime time on a certain night of the week. The YouTube algorithm also plays into how well you do on YouTube, so you have to keep it happy as well. It was a slow and steady climb for me, and still is. I think the thought process has always been focused on the quality of the content, which I've always been fully committed to.

ON KEEPING UP WITH THE CHANGES TO INSTAGRAM . . .

I don't follow any formula for Instagram although I probably should! Instagram has changed a great deal in the last year. I'm a little more strategic now about when and what I post, but I still keep the focus on the photos and videos, making sure my audience is enjoying them. If you get too caught up in strategy it will make you crazy. It doesn't matter, really, if the photos are staged or more "real," as long as I'm giving people the kind of content they want to see and also making them laugh!

ON DECIDING YOU WERE READY FOR AN AGENT . . .

Oh, boy, was I ready. I'd been negotiating my own deals for a while before being approached by Abrams. It wasn't easy! I'd been approached by one other notable agency in LA around the same time, but after I met with Jade and Alec, I decided I didn't need to meet with the other agency. The qualities I looked for in an agency were there; there was no need to explore other options.

Alec is a heavy hitter in the digital and entertainment space, and it was clear he had a vision for Abrams's alternative programming department. After that meeting I knew I wanted to be a part of it. And I was very fortunate to be paired with my agent, Jade Sherman. I just can't say enough about her and how we work together. I wouldn't be where I am without her. I'm used to being the hardest worker and the shark in any group, but Alec and Jade make me feel like I'm not doing enough! Not on purpose, of course, but I'm personally inspired by their drive and work ethic.

ON PICKING A NICHE BEFORE BRANCHING OUT . . .

I don't know that it's necessarily crucial to pick a niche and excel there first before expanding, but that's what happened with me. I was hesitant at first to cross over into fashion, because I didn't want to be seen as the "beauty girl" trying to be a fashion expert. But quickly I learned that my audience just wanted to see my personal style; there was a demand for it. That's what gave me the push to start sharing style content.

Travel was an easy one to add to my content because it allowed me to begin creating these visually beautiful narrative-style videos, which I need for my own creative satisfaction. Now, it's about diversifying the content in such a way that my audience still feels like they're not only getting what they came to me for in the first place (beauty) but getting these new and exciting videos and photos.

ON BEING AN INFLUENCER IN YOUR THIRTIES . . .

The nature of this business is such that you absolutely can get started in your thirties. The challenge is the trends: Most of what becomes trendy in social media is geared toward younger people, and sometimes it feels silly to jump on that wagon if you're not twenty-two. But that doesn't mean you can't cater to a more mature audience. If I weren't doing this full time I'd be acting, because that's what I was doing before digital took off for me. The deeper I get into this industry, though, the more I'm convinced I just want to go back to school, get more degrees . . . live the scholar life.

ON SHARING YOUR PERSONAL LIFE ON SOCIAL MEDIA . . .

I'm not totally comfortable sharing my personal life on social media. Some people are very comfortable with it; I'm just starting to get used to it. The only reason I'm okay with sharing personal details of my life is because I know it will debunk this idea that my life is perfect. I come from a fractured family, I have issues with anxiety, I have trouble maintaining a relationship. These are all things I've hesitated to share in the past, but I know there are people out there going through some of the same life issues, so if it can help people not feel alone in their struggle, that's more than enough reason for me to open up.

I make it my number one priority to always keep everything that comes out of my mouth honest and authentic, and that leaves very little room for negativity. Of course, I do get the occasional negative comment, but I just keep it moving. The people who write nasty comments don't realize how transparent they are; you just kind of feel bad for them and move on. The constructive criticism, however, is always welcomed and helps me improve my content. I keep that communication very open with my audience and I appreciate their willingness to keep it 100 with me.

ON BEING FRIENDS WITH OTHER INFLUENCERS . . .

It's always nice to have people around you who understand your challenges and what you go through day to day. It's very important to have those relationships, especially in an industry that inherently feels competitive. I've seen nothing but support and encouragement from other influencers, and I reciprocate that; it's the only way. Most of us made friends earlier on in our careers so it's been nice to see how far we've all come.

ON WOMEN DOMINATING INFLUENCER MARKETING . . .

I think it's about time women dominated an industry that sits on millions of dollars. We've created a space where we've taken our respective leads in our careers, each in our own way, and that's extremely rare. This line of work allows content creators to do practically anything we want; we make decisions that determine where our careers go. And, industry-wide, we keep a certain level of quality and professionalism that has allowed us to be taken seriously. Truly, what other industry do you know of that allows women to make the kind of living that we do? We don't focus on that fact very often, but it's monumental.

And, in turn, our role as content creators has made way for other women to have the confidence to make big moves. I don't look at any of what we do as creating unrealistic expectations; rather we are paving the way for this new and blossoming industry to become a brand-new opportunity for women and girls that wasn't available just a decade ago. It's funny, because people love to focus on the "pressures" on women. No, we can handle it. That's what we do. And that's what

I would tell young girls who want to become content creators.

ON HINDSIGHT BEING 20/20 . . .

I wish I had the confidence to fully immerse myself in the digital space without hesitation. I hesitated a lot, but I would tell aspiring influencers to confidently take a step forward knowing you have something unique to offer that no one else has.

CHAPTER 6

The Contract

How do you decipher all this legalese?

Whenever I'm booking an influencer, getting her signature on the contract is either the hardest or the easiest part.

If I'm working through the contract with her agent, manager, or lawyer, there are tons of revisions and we go back and forth until both parties are happy with the terms. But, when I send a contract directly to an influencer, it comes back so quickly I am almost certain she didn't read it. Or if she did, she didn't give it a thorough reading; it was more of a skim. Maybe it's the former law student in me, but you never, ever sign a contract without reading, and I mean really reading, it.

EXPERT TIP

Read over EVERY contract and be aware of what you are committing to, even if you have an attorney and an agent.

—Jade Sherman (@jadesherman), agent at Abrams Artists Agency

Legalese is a foreign language, so I can understand why contracts are intimidating. But if you learn the basics, you can sign on the dotted line confident that you know what you're getting into. Every contract you encounter will be different, but they should all have most of the elements that follow.

- **Personal Information.** This includes your name, phone number, mailing address, and email address. Make sure all of this information is correct, as it will be how they contact you during the campaign and how they will pay you. Now is the time to disclose if the name you've been using on Instagram isn't your legal name or if your bank account is actually in your maiden/married name. You don't want your payment delayed because of this mix-up.

- **Campaign Details.** This will lay out who is hiring you (it might be an agency, a publisher, or the advertiser directly), who you are creating content for (usually the advertiser), and what brand the content should be about (this is where you'll find the name of the product or service). This section might also include the campaign brief, but that deserves its own section, so we'll tackle it after the contract basics.

- **Shooting Schedule.** Pretty self-explanatory, the shooting schedule will have the details of the photo or video shoot. You'll look for things like date(s), city location, and shoot duration. The duration is how long you'll be on set. It could be short, like 3 hours, or much longer, like 10 hours. Keep in mind this doesn't include travel to or from the shoot (portal-to-portal) so always get a good night's sleep before a shoot and plan for a long day.

  The contract may not always have your call time or the location of the shoot because sometimes the production team is still figuring all of that out. A few days before the shoot you'll receive a call sheet, and it will have all the details, sometimes even times for breakfast and lunch. Every shoot I've ever been on has always had great food and lots of snacks and beverages. If you have any allergies or special requests (you're vegan or gluten-free), let them know. You'll want to make sure there are lots of options for you to eat.

DON'T BE THAT GIRL

Now, I shouldn't have to say this, but when you've been booked for a campaign, you're working, so you should keep personal activities to a minimum. Can you call your mom during the break? Sure. Can you text a friend how excited you are in-between looks? Why not? Can you post behind-the-scenes photos from your shoot on Instagram? Yes please, unless it's confidential. But you probably shouldn't take the car I sent and go to a doctor's appointment for two hours while we're waiting for you on set. There is no such thing as a quick doctor's appointment. Next time, for every minute you waste, we're going to send you a bill.

- **Deliverables.** This section is devoted to what you are contractually obligated to deliver for the campaign. It could be something simple, like the caption for your Instagram post, or something more complex, like providing five full-length looks using the advertiser's products and five variations of each look.

  The assets listed in this section are what the people hiring you will expect to receive before they pay you. I try to make this section as detailed as possible so there is no confusion, but you also need to read it multiple times and make sure you've delivered what I ask. One bag spill, one flat lay, and two street-style shots does not mean two bag spills and two flat lays. And it should go without saying, but your photos should be shot in a professional manner and should be edited with the same vigor you would use if it was an organic post. And they should be hi-res and shot at 300 dpi. If you don't know what that means, research it and learn it before you shoot anything. Actually, your photos should be even more spectacular than what's on your feed because you had a budget to create the content. Remember the production tips I gave you in Chapter 4? Better yet, take part of your fee and hire a professional photographer. It will show in your work and will make everyone's lives easier.

DON'T BE THAT GIRL

This story still makes my blood boil because the level of unprofessionalism was astounding.

I sent an influencer the product that she was supposed to self-shoot and then send back along with the photos. After confirming she had received the product, we waited. And waited. And waited some more. Her agent kept insisting we would have the photos by the deadline. On the day the photos were due, the agent said I would have them that night. I finally got them, and they were legit the worst photos I had ever seen. I could have given my toddler a flip phone and the photos would have been better. Some of them were on a poorly lit subway car, others were on her fire escape with the product surrounded by dead plants. I almost had a meltdown in my apartment.

Cue me calling the agent and flipping out. She promised to get me better photos from the influencer. So, I waited. And then the influencer took the product out of the country because she wanted to shoot the photos in a cool location. Sigh. What if customs confiscated it? What if it was stolen? What if the airline lost it? So many bad things could have happened, and she obviously wasn't thinking about any of them. But now I can't even get the product back, so I wait. And wait some more.

Her agent wrote me and asked for an extension. When I asked why, she said it was because the influencer was sick. Ugh. We don't want the influencer looking a haute mess in the content, so we can't really say no. Fine, she can have an extension. Days go by, and then I'm told the friends the influencer traveled with left the country and now she doesn't have anyone to shoot the photos. Why this is my problem? I don't know, but she needs another extension. I told her to go find someone with a camera, or buy one and hire someone to shoot the photos immediately. I had built a buffer into when the photos were due to the client, but now she was making me cut it close.

More days go by and I tell the agent I will ban every single person on their roster if I don't have these photos by the new deadline. Magically they arrive "on time." Our brand loves them, the client loves them, and everyone is happy. Everyone but me. I am fuming. I taped those terrible photos to my walls and told everyone who came into my office the story. It all worked out in the end, but that influencer? She's banned for life.

- **Term Summary and Flight Dates.** Some contracts will include one or both of these terms, but in a nutshell, the *term summary* is the length of the agreement. It usually starts the day you sign the contract and ends when the campaign is over. The *flight dates* are when content is live. You'll usually have a set date you need to publish your photos and you can't delete them, or archive them, until the flight is over.

- **Exclusivity.** Pay special attention to this section, because it will dictate who you cannot work with and for how long. Sometimes it will be an advertiser's top three or five competitors and they will tell you who is included. Other times it will be category exclusivity, in which case you cannot work with anyone in that category (lipstick, beer, paint, sunglasses, department stores, etc.).

When discussing length of exclusivity, it could be one week, one month, three months, or longer. The most important thing to remember is once you agree to exclusivity, it is set in stone. It doesn't matter if you sign a deal with a perfume company for $2,500 for three months and two months in one of their competitors offers you $100,000 for a one-year deal. You cannot work with them until your exclusivity is up, and if that causes you to miss out on $100,000, that's the way it will need to be. Unless of course you or your agent ask the advertiser for permission and it is granted. This is why in Chapter 5, I kept telling you to request more details or a contract before you formally accept because the devil is in the details.

Extended exclusivity should definitely cause you to increase your price. I'm a firm believer that one-month exclusivity inclusive of an advertiser's top three competitors is fair. Anything over that should make the price go up. Exclusivity during holidays (like Mother's Day and Valentine's Day) and specialty seasons should also increase your price because advertisers throw around money like candy during these periods and you'll have to decline more deals than normal. The high seasons vary depending on your niche, but the top five are:

- Holiday: Thanksgiving–New Year's Day
- Back-to-School: August–September (Big for mom influencers)
- Fashion Week: Fall + Spring (Big for fashion and beauty)
- Prom (Big for influencers with a teen audience)
- January (Big for fitness and health/wellness influencers)

You'll be able to decide how much to increase your price by how much interest you've been receiving. If you're just starting out, you can be much more flexible than if brands are blowing up your inbox day and night. What should you do if you have a few offers lingering from competitors, but no firm contracts? The same thing you would do if you had more than one job offer. Write everyone and let them know you have another offer that would keep you from working with them and see if they want to make you a better one. If not, you can sign with confidence and not piss off anyone in the process.

- **Usage.** Usage is another one of those things that people always make harder than it should be. Usage dictates what the advertisers are allowed to do with your photos/videos. Whether you took them yourself, or the brand/advertiser took them of you, your image is worth something, and you have to protect it. Standard usage covers the advertiser posting the photos/videos on their owned and operated (O&O) digital channels. This means their website, blog, and social media channels. You should make sure they're giving you credit or mentioning your name/handle wherever they share it.

Other types of usage include:

- **Paid Social**. Where they will turn your content into ads on Facebook, Instagram, and Twitter
- **Pre-Roll**. The mini-commercials before a video, usually seen on YouTube
- **In-book**. An advertisement in a print magazine
- **In-store**. Signage in a store
- **POS**. Point of sale/at a checkout station
- **Third-Party**. Ads run through a company like Nativo. You know when you see ads in the middle of a page or links to other articles at the end of a post? Those are third-party ads.

As with exclusivity, additional usage should cause your price to go up, because it increases the chance competitors will see your content, associate you with that brand, and not hire you for an upcoming campaign. But as with all requests from a brand, keep in mind your current opportunities and what you stand to gain from the one in front of you. You wouldn't want to price yourself out because of exclusivity or usage when it could be the beginning of a great relationship with XYZ brand or agency. If you're affordable and do a great job, they will keep coming back to you, and you'll make more money. I've used @colormecourtney at least three times because she is lovely, professional, and always works with me on budget. That's not to say she is cheap, because she's definitely not, but she's pleasant and always worth her fee.

- **Payment.** This may be the most important section of any contract because this is where the money is discussed. For the most part, you'll see the following elements regarding payment:

  - **Fee**. How much they are paying you. This may or may not have changed from the number in the soft offer depending on what the final terms were.
  - **Payment Terms**. This will say something like "net 30" or "net 60." This is how long they have to pay you after you submit your

invoice. When negotiating your fee, if their proposed fee is lower than you'd like and they can't budge on money, there may be some wiggle room around the payment terms. Maybe you can be paid a percentage up front and a percentage after the campaign is over. Maybe the payment terms can be changed to net 30 when they originally proposed net 45. It's quite possible that the final offer is the best they can do, but it never hurts to ask. I want this to be a rewarding experience for both of us so, as long as an influencer is polite when she asks, I will try my best to accommodate whatever requests I can.

- **Paperwork.** you'll usually have to send an invoice (make sure it has your name, address, and campaign details on it), your W9, and some sort of payment form. Some companies still pay influencers by check, but most pay by direct deposit, so you'll need an ACH form like the one you would give your employer and a voided check. There may be a few companies that pay by PayPal or Venmo, but they're usually small and scrappy companies that aren't paying thousands of different people.

- **Travel and Expenses.** If the campaign requires travel, this section outlines how the influencer will get to the shoot and who is responsible for booking and paying for travel. In most cases, all travel arrangements are taken care of by the casting agent. To be honest, it's the least favorite part of my job. Booking travel for influencers is always a beast. Not just because booking travel is annoying in general, but because there are quite a few influencers who think they are entitled to better accommodations than they actually are.

  Unless you have 500,000 followers on Instagram or 500,000 subscribers on YouTube, do not even think about asking to fly business class. Yes, I know about JetBlue Mint, and no, I do not care that it's sometimes only a little more expensive than economy. We book through our corporate travel agent and when I need to book a business-class ticket, very important people have to sign off on it, so the influencer better be worth it. But unless you fall into the category of celebrity or high-end model, under no circumstances are you allowed to ask to be flown first class.

I would even encourage top-tier influencers to agree to fly economy and then upgrade themselves. They travel so much, they probably have points they can use to upgrade. In the end, they would wind up ahead. They would probably get larger fees, because we would need a smaller budget for their travel. And they'd get booked more because they are so easy to work with. Certainly, not all influencers are divas, but some of them really let the numbers go to their head. There's this one influencer who needed to stay at a particular hotel, in a specific room with a certain tub, and wanted an allowance for juice and midnight snacks. I am sorry, I wasn't aware I booked a kindergartener for this campaign . . .

DON'T BE THAT GIRL

I was once booking an influencer and we were discussing the terms. Her manager got testy with me when I told her we could fly her client business class since she has over 1MM followers on Instagram. She then told me her client only flew first class. I laughed so hard I practically ruined my laptop with all the water I spit out onto it.

The influencer wanted to fly first class? As if she were an actual famous person? The manager then continued to babble on about how her client couldn't fly business because people would recognize her. I'm sorry but who is fangirling over a beauty YouTuber in business class? And if she is so famous, surely she flies first class on her own dollar and should have the points to upgrade herself?

Needless to say, I didn't book the influencer, and I avoid that manager like the plague. And the sad part is there are probably a bunch of great girls on her roster who don't even know why I won't book them.

FTC RULES AND REGULATIONS

The Federal Trade Commission (FTC) is an independent agency of the US government dedicated to protecting America's consumers. Or as I like to call them, the #ad police. When it comes to influencer marketing, they want to make sure that when people see a post on an influencer's blog or social media channels, they know whether or not that influencer has been compensated for the post. And we appreciate that. I mean, who wants to run out and buy a lipstick on a vlogger's recommendation, only to find out that the lipstick is terrible and the influencer only promoted it because she was paid to?

Now, for the most part, influencers don't mislead their audiences, because if they recommend bad products, they'll lose credibility with them. I have worked with many influencers who will make me send them a product (or go out and buy it themselves, if it is available in stores), so they can try it before they sign on to a campaign. I love these types of influencers, because it means that if they say yes, they're actually into the product and won't just be giving lip service.

The FTC really wants the disclaimer to be as large and in charge as possible, but there are easy ways to properly disclose without stamping a big dollar sign on your content.

- **Blog and Vlog.** You definitely should start your blog post off letting your readers know you partnered with XYZ brand. If your content is always good, they won't stop reading/watching because it's sponsored; they'll keep going because they want to see the amazing content you've created with production dollars! You can also make your title something like *XYZ Collab: 9 Items You Need in Your Closet for Fall,* or on your blog create a category called "Partnerships" or "Collaborations." That way there won't be any doubt an advertiser put dollars behind your content.

On YouTube, in addition to the mention in the title and description, you also need to call out that this is a sponsored video in the actual video. Something simple like "Hey guys, welcome back to my channel. Today I'm going to show you the goods from my haul. Shout out to XYZ brand for partnering with me and making this video happen" should suffice and will also make the brand happy to get a mention so early in the video.

- **Facebook and Instagram.** While I was writing this book, Instagram changed their disclosure policy to be the same as Facebook's. Before, on Instagram you just needed to have a nice #ad in your caption, although many influencers also use #sp, #sponsored, and #partner (even though

> the FTC doesn't like those disclaimers). But now, if they have the tool, influencers must tag XYZ brand and it will be clear as day to all audience members that this post was created as part of a paid partnership. It definitely takes the guesswork out of disclosing and there's no way to get around it. It will be included in your contract, and if Facebook/Instagram catch you trying to skirt around the disclosure, they can hide your post and even ban you from the platform.

I will never understand why influencers have issues disclosing they were paid by a brand. If your audience wants you to keep making content full-time, then you're going to need to make a full-time salary. Also, if you're keeping to the 70/30 rule, then they also shouldn't be tired of seeing ads on your feed. And finally, if you are using that money to make better content than what you create on your own, they will be stoked to see what you come up with for each collaboration.

CAMPAIGN BRIEF

Earlier, when I was talking about the contract, I said that it may contain a campaign brief. Here's the lowdown on what that actually is.

There's a joke in the advertising world that briefs are never brief and this is 100 percent true. They're always fifteen pages long and have pie charts, graphs, and other visual aids. They're a pain in the butt to create, but when you're an influencer, receiving a good brief is priceless.

Think of the brief as creative direction from the brand. They definitely want you to create content in your own style, but they need to make sure it is on brand for them as well. A brief may tell you that XYZ's target consumer is eighteen to twenty-one years old, so don't create content that is too juvenile or too mature. A lingerie company might say you must always have on a shirt or bathrobe when showcasing their bra. A liquor company will tell you that you cannot have any motor vehicles in your content and should not even hint at the fact that you may be driving.

The brief will usually tell you the history of the brand, give you details on the product, and include talking points like sale dates, sizes, price points, ingredients, etc. Briefs come in all shapes and sizes and the only thing you really need to remember is to READ IT. If you do not follow the directions in the brief and you submit content that does not comply, the brand can make you reshoot everything or they can refuse to pay you. The brief may also include submission deadlines. If you do not submit your content on time, the brand can refuse to pay you and may never work with you ever again. Bottom line is, if you don't follow instructions you don't get paid, and how sad would it be, if after all that work, you didn't get paid because you didn't read the brief?

INFLUENCER ICON

ALEXANDRA PEREIRA

@lovelypepa + lovelypepa.com

Alexandra was on a path to become a lawyer when she decided to switch gears and launch her blog in 2009. The legal world's loss was our gain, because she has one of the best Instagrams most English and Spanish speakers have the pleasure of following. She is tiny, but has a huge personality and joie de vivre, and it's no surprise that her motto is "Stay hungry. Stay foolish." When she's not in an airport or packing luggage, she's working on her clothing line, the Lovely Pepa Collection, which is inspired by landscapes, evolving style, and wanderlust.

ON BECOMING A BLOGGER . . .

Becoming a blogger started out as a hobby. I was inspired and fascinated by other people blogging and logged onto several blogs every day. I was hooked and quite taken by the idea of it. So one night, while hanging out at home, I thought to myself: Why shouldn't I start one of my own? And this is how I embarked on this whole adventure. Little did I know how this moment would later define the course of my life.

When it comes to what I wanted to share with the world, it was pretty clear to me that it had to be fashion. It was the topic I was most passionate about, and I felt I had something to share with others. I started posting my everyday looks alongside bits and pieces of my life and people loved it!

Pepa is my French bulldog. She's the one who inspired the name of the blog. I thought that the name would sound nicer if I added an English component to it. I thought the mix of both English and Spanish had a nice sound to it.

ON LEANING MORE INTO YOUR YOUTUBE CHANNEL . . .

Although my YouTube account is several years old, I only began to consistently post on my channel in August 2017. I felt like it was an important step for me, as it allowed my followers to have a different type of interaction with me, one that would allow them to know me better.

My first videos were junk and I discarded them; I didn't think the quality was good enough, and I only like to release works that I feel have been done properly. YouTube is a world that is totally different from Instagram. It is much more real, and I would say that in some cases, much more useful. The YouTube crowd is typically more engaged. They almost always leave longer comments than I would see on Instagram or other social media platforms.

ON SPEAKING TWO LANGUAGES ON YOUR PLATFORMS . . .

Spanish and English are two of the most widespread languages in the world, and this represents an opportunity to connect with a huge amount of people. Creating content in various languages should be motivated by exactly that: connecting with more people so that you increase the chances of people appreciating your content.

However, that does come with an extra load of work, and it is easy to burn yourself out. My recommendation to aspiring multilingual influencers would be to study this kind of move carefully before investing themselves in it. Once it is done, it will be hard to go back on it.

For example, my Spanish-speaking followers know me in Spanish and love me for that. If I ever stopped communicating in that language, I would alienate a lot of them and I would risk losing their interest.

ON PRODUCING HIGH-QUALITY CONTENT . . .

In my opinion, the key to maintaining a steady stream of high-quality content is to prepare it some days before it gets published. My team and I brainstorm about content production on a daily basis. We'll think about how to coordinate travel, locations, and outfits so that they come together in the most inspiring, engaging, and aesthetic way. Everything has to come together in the right place at the right time. I guess, one key to our success is maintaining the right balance between all these elements. However, it is important to know that no matter how prepared you are, a more spontaneous and genuine approach also works. Some of our most popular posts have been ones we hadn't planned for.

As far as sponsored content is concerned, it does not differ from content we would create organically. I am very careful to maintain a genuine and consistent identity throughout my feed, and creative freedom is a nonnegotiable condition that I require before starting a relationship with a brand.

ON TRAVELING SO OFTEN . . .

It is quite complicated to live like I do, but I find it enjoyable, and I've adapted quite well to this lifestyle. When I stop traveling, I feel like something is not right. I've become addicted to discovering new places and still get as excited about it as when I went on my first trip (which was to Disneyland when I was five).

Maintaining a steady stream of content requires preparing content in advance. I typically leave four to five days of margin before publishing. Sometimes, I have to be flexible about it, especially if I have a contractual obligation to publish something that is time sensitive. However, the general rule is that we spend at least four days editing the material, and those who work with us usually comply with our modus operandi. They even encourage it, as they would prefer that the content they sponsor be of high quality and benefit from a better response from our followers.

ON SWITCHING CAREERS FROM LAW TO DESIGN AND CONTENT . . .

I think I knew law wasn't for me a few weeks after I started the program. Still, I kept at it as I thought it was the safest bet for my future. But the best thing I ever did was to switch careers.

I highly encourage people to overcome any fears they have and pursue something they are truly passionate about, something that gives purpose to their life. Closing a door opens new opportunities, and when it comes down to it, every problem has a solution. It is all about defining the problem and thinking on the solution.

I do not regret not becoming a lawyer. I do believe that if I stuck to my original plan, I would've been a mediocre lawyer and led an unexciting life. Therefore, starting my blog was the best thing I ever did.

ON WORKING WITH YOUR SIGNIFICANT OTHER . . .

Working with my partner, like anything else, has its benefits and challenges. We decided to work together because I believed he had skills that strongly complemented mine. He has a strong business background and organizational skills while I am more of a creative sort. He has overhauled our whole activity into a real business, while I get to focus on delivering more content through more platforms and in higher quality.

When it comes to working with a life partner, I believe there are no clear rules that can determine whether such a relationship can be successful or not. I believe the most important thing is to draw a clear separation between work and home so as to not let one take over the other. It is my belief that it is this balance that is the foundation of a successful and healthy work relationship with a significant other.

ON TAKING IT TO THE NEXT LEVEL AND DESIGNING YOUR OWN LINE . . .

Sometimes I have to pinch myself and remind myself that I'm actually doing this. It is truly a dream come true! I had thought about launching my own line for a long time and I wanted it to be the next step I took in my career. Therefore, when all the right conditions presented themselves, I didn't think about it twice and immediately went for the opportunity. Obviously, this would have not been possible without the success of Lovely Pepa. Pooled together, my blog and social media reach millions, and leveraging that power of influence is at the core of our business model.

ON WOMEN DOMINATING INFLUENCER MARKETING . . .

I am quite encouraged by this achievement, as the professional world usually works against women. It is proof that sex does not determine your ability to be successful at a job, and it is high time that we started being valued for our ability to get a job done rather than other considerations.

The Insta-ready lifestyle should not create unrealistic expectations for women out there. Sometimes, I believe that by aiming to inspire others, we can also end up relaying a misleading message: that something is wrong with who you are. In that sense, I believe that we bear the responsibility to keep our public aware of the reality and imperfections behind this picture-perfect world that we have built.

My advice to young content creators is to make an educated decision about pursuing this kind of lifestyle. This path is complicated and not perfect. We have our bad days just like everyone else. Also, we work every day of the week; I do not know what a weekend means.

ON HINDSIGHT BEING 20/20 . . .

I would have loved to have a mentor when I first started—someone from this industry to talk to about the issues I faced and that would actually understand and guide me in my choices and on how to maintain the right life-work balance. Social interaction is also very important, and our lifestyle can also come at the cost of our relationships.

As far as aspiring influencers are concerned, I would say that most importantly, you should believe in yourself. If you do it right, you can achieve success. This will come with hard work and by making sacrifices along the way. But nothing good ever comes for free. Most importantly, I recommend you embrace what makes you different, for it is what will eventually make your brand.

CHAPTER 7

The Agent

How do you know when you're ready and where do you find one?

You might be wondering how your favorite influencer books all of these campaigns while still finding time to create amazing content. The short answer is, she doesn't. She probably has a team of people helping her on the business side so she can focus on the creative.

Many influencers who are at the top of the industry have assembled a squad that includes one to all of the big five.

1. **The Assistant.** She answers emails, books travel, and keeps an eye on the editorial calendar. She usually is paid hourly. Or she may be your mom, who is super happy you're finally off her couch.

2. **The Manager.** She gives you career advice, keeps tabs on the other members of your squad, and helps you expand your brand into makeup lines, fashion collaborations, and collections at Target. Many influencer managers were previously accountants or lawyers, so they often help their clients with those areas as well. She usually makes a percentage (15 to 20 percent) of your yearly income, so it's in her best interest to make sure you are successful.

3. **The Publicist.** She keeps you in the public eye and finds media opportunities to raise your profile. She usually works on retainer, so you pay her X amount of dollars for X amount of hours. She wants you to do well, because if you don't, you won't have any money to pay her and you'll have to let her go.

4. **The Attorney.** She goes over all your contracts and negotiates your terms. She also makes sure your exclusivity windows don't overlap. She usually charges an insane amount per hour and you pay her, because no matter how much she costs, it's still less than settling a lawsuit.

5. **The Agent.** She sometimes does all the above depending on the size of the company she works for, or if she owns her own agency. She's here to make sure you book campaigns, because she doesn't get paid unless you do. She usually makes 10 to 15 percent of each deal she gets you, although in California she's capped at 10 percent. She is the most important person on this list, so we're going to spend the rest of the chapter talking about her.

THE GOOD, THE BAD, AND THE UGLY

Agents are my people, because I spend all day talking to them on the phone, emailing them between meetings, and having lunch with them to talk about everything from brand fails to our favorite influencers.

Agents are a great asset, because they're in constant contact with people who are in a position to offer you money. I was working on a campaign and needed to secure a fabulous teenager who was great in front of the camera. And I needed to do it quickly, because the shoot was less than a week away. I searched Instagram and YouTube for days and found a lot of girls that I liked but none that I loved for this particular advertiser. Jade over at Abrams told me I should look at rising star Daniella Perkins (@daniellaperkins), and she was exactly what I was looking for. Super cute, great smile, amazing personality, and acting chops. I loved her, the editor loved her, and the advertiser loved her. A win for everyone involved, and I never would have found her in time on my own.

But for every three agents that I love, there is one that drives me crazy—and here are the top five reasons why.

1. **She doesn't respond to emails or phone calls in a timely manner.** When your entire job consists of emails and phone calls to book jobs for your clients and you don't do either, you're a terrible agent. Although I hate when agents don't respond when I put out a soft offer, I can deal with it. But when we're in the middle of a negotiation and she disappears for three days, or we have a shoot/deadline coming up and she's radio silent, I might simply decide her clients aren't worth the stress she causes and stop working with her.

2. **She's fighting with me over $5.** Working through contracts with agents is far from my favorite thing, and it's because some of them don't know when they have a good deal and should just sign on the dotted line. I totally understand that they are trying to get the best deal for

their client and that the more the deal is worth, the more they make, but if you keep asking for rope, soon it will be long enough to kill this deal.

DON'T BE THAT GIRL

I was working with an agent on a pretty large budget campaign where they originally wanted $100,000, but there was no way the influencer was worth that much, so I said no. Plus, I didn't have that much money, but there was no reason for them to know that.

We finally landed on $75,000 and were ready to draw up a contract, but the agent had one last request: I also needed to fly out a sitter for the influencer's dog. Wait, what now? I am going to pay this girl $75,000 and she can't find someone to watch her dog while she flies to New York for two days? I said no and told her my budget was maxed out. Now maybe her client was a super huge diva and actually demanded this, but then the agent should have paid it out of her $7,500 commission. She probably thought I was bluffing and told me that unless I flew out the dog sitter, the deal was off. Well guess what, the deal was off.

I could almost hear her freak out from across the country via email when she realized that I wasn't bluffing, but I literally had zero dollars left. Imagine having to tell your client you just lost them $67,500 over a $675 plane ticket?

3. **She says the influencer isn't interested when I know she is because I asked her myself.** Sometimes I think agents forget that before they signed their client, other people had worked with them. I know a lot of influencers and I knew many of them when they had less than 100K followers. I also gave a lot of them their first campaign or introduced them to their agent, so we're cool like that. I often have coffee with influencers to see what they've been up to, where they're traveling next, and if there are any brands they want to work with. And I keep all the information in a database, so if an opportunity comes up I know to pitch her.

Every so often, a brand that an influencer mentioned at our coffee date comes across my desk and I'll reach out to the influencer's agent to see if she's available to do the campaign. The agent might tell me the advertiser isn't on brand for the influencer so she's going to pass. I'll know this to be BS and tell the agent to ask the influencer anyway. Lo and behold, the influencer wants to do it and we can start the negotiations.

4. **She makes extra requests after we have already settled on a fee.** Few things grind my gears more than an agent throwing a wrench into a perfectly negotiated plan. If we have hammered out all the details and come to a price that makes both parties happy, there should be very few things that flip over the whole table and make us start over. But there are some agents who forget things until the worst possible moment to remember them.

DON'T BE THAT GIRL

I did a contract where we finally settled on a fee after a few days of negotiation. I start drafting the contract and the agent just casually lets it drop that the influencer also needs to fly business class. And then she later asks if the influencer can stay at a particular hotel. Ma'am, I would have given you a whole lot less money if I knew I was going to be coughing up an extra $3,500 for travel expenses. I couldn't even say no because this influencer was the advertiser's first choice and I had already told them she would do it. If my budget is tight, I now know this agent is NOT a good one to be working with because she'll run up a tab and leave me with the bill.

5. **She says an influencer isn't available without double-checking with the influencer.**

   Max over at Buchwald is one of my favorite agents. His clients love him because he brings every offer to them and allows them to be involved in the decision making. I love this approach because why should someone else stop you from getting a paycheck? Maybe you normally wouldn't work with XYZ brand, but they just hired your favorite celeb to be their spokesperson so you're down. Or maybe they have terrible mascaras, but you're a huge fan of their eyeliner. People change their minds all the time, so your agent should never decline a campaign on your behalf unless it's for exclusivity reasons.

DON'T BE THAT GIRL

I remember emailing an influencer and her agent about a campaign I was booking. I really wanted this influencer to be a part of the campaign, but we had a tight schedule and it had to shoot on a certain date. Her agent responded quickly, telling me they would have to pass because his client would be out of the country on vacation during the shoot. Before I could even respond, the influencer jumped in and said that she would come back early so she could participate. Her agent almost lost her $10,000 because he thought she wouldn't want to cut her vacation short. Obviously her agent didn't realize $10,000 is enough money to make almost anyone get back to work.

FINDING THE ONE

There are plenty of things an agent can do that will jeopardize your career, so it's super important that you pick the right one. Whether they approach you, or you approach them, this is a defining moment of your career, so treat finding an agent the same way you would treat researching a company before accepting a job offer.

LOOK AT THEIR FULL CLIENT ROSTER

Are you focused on beauty, but all their clients are in fashion? Do you consider yourself a "relatable" influencer but their clients are more aspirational? Are you a blogger, but their roster has way more vloggers on it? These are all good questions to ask yourself and ask your potential agent. It can be both a blessing and a curse to be very different from everyone on the roster.

If anyone is looking for a plus-sized blogger and you're the only one on their list, they will pitch you each and every time. However, many agents spend time making connections with people who align with their client base. So, if their roster is full of travel bloggers, they may not be that well-connected in the home decor space. It's also important to remember that agents try to pitch their rosters in package deals, which means you will probably find yourself on the same campaigns with some of their other clients. If you take a look at the roster and on it are girls you would not want to be caught dead in the same room with, that's probably not the agency for you. But if their roster is packed with girls who are #contentgoals for you, then ding, ding, ding, you have a winner!

MEET YOUR AGENT IN REAL LIFE

I know quite a few people who chatted with their agent over email and then just signed with them. I think a few of those relationships turned out okay, but that just sounds scary to me. This is the person who will be pitching you and negotiating on your behalf. You should definitely meet them or at least video chat and see if you vibe with them.

ASK TO SPEAK WITH OTHER CLIENTS

The best way to find out what an agent is like is to speak with the other people they represent. You can ask questions about the agent's communication style and if they're generally happy with the campaigns the agent has been securing. You can also ask other clients if they've been approached by other agents, and if they have, why they've stayed.

ASK TO SEE THE CONTRACT

We've talked about how important it is to see all the details before accepting a campaign offer, and this is no different. What percentage of your earnings are they going to take? How often are you going to get paid? What does the process look like? Some agencies get paid by the advertiser and then pay you. Others let the advertiser break up their invoices into two parts and pay you directly. I've heard that there are agencies that make you wait until you earn a certain amount before they'll cut a check for you, but I've never actually seen this in action. If the agency you're considering has this as a practice, take a good long look at that number, because it might mean you will be working a lot before you see a single dime.

LOOK UP THEIR WORK HISTORY

How long have they been at this particular agency? How long have they been in this business in general? Are they well connected or are they relatively new to the game? If you're still a small fry (250K followers and under) when you land an agent, it would make sense that you'll be assigned to someone more junior, but you should still do your due diligence and stalk her out on

LinkedIn. While you're over there, check out the profiles of her coworkers and the founders AND do a deep Google search (like read the results on page 5). You'll be able to gauge her authority level and decide if she's the right person for you.

INFLUENCER INSIGHT

After being a digital content creator and brand influencer for about three years, I took the next step and signed with an agent. I had been looking for one for about a year or so and had a few reach out to me, but none of them felt like the right fit. However, when Brittany introduced me to Besidone Amoruwa, I knew she was the one right away.

There were a few things that helped me make my decision. First, I knew and trusted Brittany's suggestion since she pitched me for my first partnership at Hearst with Elle.com and Maybelline, and she had years of experience in the industry. Then, once I met Besidone in person, I connected with her on a personal level right away and trusted her. It is so important to have an agent who has your best interests in mind and really wants to help you grow personally, financially, and as a brand.

My agent also had a lot of experience working with different brands and talents, and I knew how valuable that was. She also told me that not only would she help to negotiate my contracts and partnerships, but she would be pitching me as well!

Having an agent really helped me get to the next level, open me up to opportunities I wouldn't have had otherwise, and helped me to excel as an influencer. I am super grateful to have one and I definitely suggest having an agent if possible!

—**@heygorjess**

WILL YOU BE MY AGENT?

All of this is assuming agents are blowing up your DMs trying to get you to sign with them. But what if you want to pitch yourself to an agent?

KNOW THEIR NICHE

Every agency will have a website where you can check out the type of talent they represent, and some even list their roster. If they don't, a quick Google search will help you figure out who some of their key people are. If a company only represents mommy bloggers and you are years away from having a kid, they're probably not the agency for you. But if you have access to their roster and you think you can help them fill a certain niche, that's a great thing to note.

FIND THE BEST PERSON TO CONTACT

Many companies have someone who is the head of talent, and that's who you'll want to pitch. Can't find her? An email to the CEO will usually make its way to the right person. An even better way to make contact is to be introduced by a mutual friend. That's where all this networking comes in. Surely you know *someone* who can vouch for you and tell this agency how lucky they would be to have you as a client? Social networks are a great resource to work backward from and see who can introduce you to someone you're looking to meet. Find that person and offer them 10 percent of your first campaign. Referral incentives go a long way! If you don't know anyone, it's time to start hitting the conference circuit. And if you live in a small town and these conferences are out of reach, have no fear, a well-written cold email can go a long way. I have taken meetings with and booked people who wrote me out of the blue. If you are talented, only a fool would pass without seeing what you have to offer first.

PUT YOUR BEST FOOT FORWARD

Now is the time to cue up those press materials we made in Chapter 4. A nice intro email telling the agent who you are, why you'd be a great addition to their roster, and links to your blog, social media accounts, one-sheet, and press kit will suffice. Spell their name right, get the company correct, and make sure your email is short and sweet and that all the links work. Also tell them you'll be following up in two weeks to see if there is any interest. They may be busy, but so are you, and every minute you don't have an agent, some other girl is booking a campaign that was meant for you!

EXPERT TIP

I look for engaging content and content that I personally want to watch. Influencers should reach out to agents; it's very easy to find an agent's email and shoot a quick personal email. It should not be a mass email, but something that is specific to that agent (mention other clients, specific deals, etc.). Make sure to include links to your platforms!

—Jade Sherman (@jadesherman), agent at Abrams Artists Agency

INFLUENCER ICON

CARA SANTANA

@caraasantana + caradisclothed.com

You probably recognize Cara Santana from Santa Clarita Diet *on Netflix with Drew Barrymore or* Salem *or* CSI: Crime Scene Investigation. *You might have also seen her living her best life with Jesse Metcalfe on Instagram. Or maybe you've downloaded The Glam App, a not-so-little company she created to provide women with luxury on-demand beauty services. Regardless of where you know her from, she is taking over the world and looking absolutely stunning while doing so.*

ON BLOGGING AS A SECOND CAREER . . .

I never made a decision, per se, to become a blogger. At the point in time that I launched CaraDisclothed, I was getting a lot of attention for what I was wearing. Through my relationship and the media interest, my style became a focal point with young women in particular. I loved the idea of having an open dialogue with other women about style.

As an actress, what you wear and the impression you communicate with your aesthetic is one of the first aspects of developing a character. So for me, fashion goes hand in hand with my career as an actress. Ultimately, the industry evolved, and influencing via the digital platforms has become big business. I love that girls have become editors of their own online magazines, aka a blog, and have direct access to consumers who are invested in what they wear. The name of my blog came from a friend. It was a play on words and how to dissect and strip down what you wear to what it means or says about you.

ON PRODUCING HIGH-QUALITY CONTENT . . .

The one thing you have over anyone else is your point of view, your individuality. So I always ask myself, "Is what I do intrinsic to my identity?" If it's not, I don't do it. You have to stay true to yourself. Audiences are discerning these days, and if you aren't genuine, people see right through that. So that's first and foremost.

Second, know what you're good at and what your weaknesses are. And once you've identified that, find someone whose strengths are your weaknesses. I, for one, cannot edit photos, so I hire someone (Karen Rosalie) who gets my aesthetic and curates my content's editing to fit. There is no shame in that. It's a big business, and no one runs a successful business on their own.

And last, there is more power in no than yes. Stand your ground, maintain your value, and know your worth. Saying no only builds your stock.

ON TRAVELING SO OFTEN . . .

Being on the road is both a blessing and a curse. I love the experience of traveling and being exposed to new and different cultures and experiences, however, it can be lonely and tough at times. I usually travel with my assistant to ensure I'm able to maintain my workload as I also am the founder and CEO of The Glam App and an actress, and I sometimes bring my photographer. I love traveling with my fiancé, and whenever I can, I bring my dogs so I don't get too homesick.

In the event that I have a heavy workload, I shoot content in advance. I'm typically working with six weeks of content, so I'm never without. We have a working editorial calendar so there is a lot of methodology to what I have lined up. I also try to balance my schedule as much as possible so I don't burn out or get too tired. There's a lot that goes into this job. From coordination with agent, manager, and publicist to scheduling, photography, etc.—it really is a machine.

ON POSTING CONTENT WITH YOUR FIANCÉ, ACTOR JESSE METCALFE . . .

Most people think I don't post him enough. There's definitely a balance of not exploiting the relationship, maintaining some anonymity as an actress, and still engaging with people in an authentic way. I try to let it be genuine without making it the focal point of my story. As with everything, it's really strategic. But if I do post Jesse, he has approved the photo! Ha ha.

ON TAKING IT TO THE NEXT LEVEL AND FOUNDING THE GLAM APP . . .

I didn't have a background in beauty, tech, business, finance, or anything else that would really go along with building a business. That being said, I worked hard, I focused on the goal, and I asked for advice and expertise where I needed it. Building a team around me who all have strong areas of skill was fundamentally important, and not being afraid to fail was a huge part of it. If I had known what it would take, I never would have done it, so my naïveté paid off. But as it's grown, I've made it a point to apply myself and learn what I originally did not know.

I think my biggest piece of advice to anyone venturing out and starting a business is focus on what it is you are trying to do, your mission statement. From there, surround yourself with people who balance your abilities and don't take your criticism personally, but take it seriously. Life and business is an evolution and you have to be open to the journey.

ON WOMEN DOMINATING INFLUENCER MARKETING . . .

I love that women dominate the field. It's one of the only business arenas we do! I'm proud of my friends and colleagues who have paved the way to create this sustainable and profitable business for themselves. They are entrepreneurs, businesswomen, and they are creative, expressive, and thoughtful while doing something they love.

Of course, living your life through the camera lens can cause a distortion of reality, which is why it's important to balance the truth and fiction. I see a lot of women making a point to show a more full and realistic version of their life. However, we are artists, content creators, and just like making a movie, you cut out the parts that aren't the best, and that doesn't make it disingenuous. People want to see aspirational imagery, and we—both the influencers and society at large—have the responsibility to educate young women on realistic goals and expectations. Art and commerce have always required balance.

ON HINDSIGHT BEING 20/20 . . .

Looking back, I would tell my younger self, "Don't compare yourself, don't judge yourself—be yourself!"

PART 4

Planning Your Future

CHAPTER 8

The Goal

How do you prepare for what's next?

Once you're a bona fide influencer you'll constantly be asking yourself what's next. In an industry where you're only as good as your last six posts, you must always be on the lookout for ways to stand out to advertisers and increase the value of your personal brand. There are three steps to a long-term career as an influencer, and in this closing chapter we'll talk through getting repeat business, securing long-term campaigns and ambassadorships, and starting your own business.

When working with an influencer on a campaign, I am happy when she does the bare minimum: answering emails in a timely manner, producing beautiful content or being pleasant on a photoshoot, and providing all deliverables/posting on time. But you know who my favorite influencers are? The ones that I've booked over and over?

They're the influencers that went the extra mile. I've never thought "underpromise and overdeliver" was a good business motto, but they were definitely onto something with the "overdeliver" part.

A few months ago I was checking my mail at work, not my email, my physical mail from the post office, when I found a thank-you letter from an influencer I had booked. It was such a lovely note and I put it right next to the two other thank-you notes I had received. I have booked hundreds of influencers and I have received exactly three thank-you notes. Three. Now do you have to send a thank-you note? Of course not. But should you? Absolutely. If all other things are equal, I am pushing for the influencer who sent the thank-you note each and every time.

Something as small as a note can light up someone's day, so imagine the points you score when you provide advertisers with extra content they didn't pay for. I have busted out an entire dance routine in the office when this happens, and the influencer barely had to do extra work. Here are a few examples:

- **Provide us with a mood board.** When you're figuring out what to shoot for a campaign, you're planning it all out anyway. You have inspiration for hair, makeup, clothing, and location. A mood board is a document that shows the reader your vision for the shoot. Is it inspired by a happy California beach girl or is it grittier and inspired by New York Street style? It helps everyone get on the same page and allows for any course correction if you're missing the mark. I'll never forget when I hired @scoutthecity for a campaign and she sent back a mood board before she started shooting. I shared it with the client and not only were they thrilled, but they booked her directly for a future campaign.

- **Take and send extra photos.** If I ask you to send six looks for a campaign and you send eight, you've automatically made everyone's life easier. Not only will my team have more photos to choose from, but we can also tell the advertiser we were able to get them two extra looks at the same price. If you're posting content on your own pages and you can throw in an extra blog post, do it. Maybe the listicle they hired you to do was "One Dress Five Ways" but you could also make a listicle called "Seven Things I Pack on Every Trip" and make the dress one of them. You were already doing that article, but now you've given an advertiser an extra plug. No one is going to be angry about that.

- **Throw in an extra post or an Instagram Story.** I'll usually contract an influencer for one post, because anything more than that is usually outside my budget. But takeovers are the crème de la crème of Instagram activations. A takeover is when an influencer posts three photos/videos in a row. It's called a takeover because the brand has "taken over" the top row of the influencer's feed, and if it sounds expensive, that's because it is. So imagine my delight when an influencer is only obligated to post once, but she posts three times. Now, such posts don't need to be an official part of the campaign, but you can work them into your regularly scheduled content. I once hired an influencer for a purse activation. She posted the official photo, but she also posted an organic photo of herself wearing the purse out on the town and one at a restaurant with her purse on the table. The client absolutely lost their minds and sent her a purse to keep. Sometimes you don't have room to add in extra posts, but don't worry—Instagram Stories are just as good. An influencer I hired for a campaign did a random, nonbranded story wearing the advertiser's dress and they made me

> promise to include her every time they ran a campaign. A free bag and guaranteed work for a few posts? The influencer definitely came out on top in both of these scenarios.

LET'S MAKE IT OFFICIAL

You might be wondering, *When is the best time to talk to an advertiser about a long-term partnership?* The answer to that is while the success of your last campaign is still fresh in their minds. If you've fulfilled your contractual obligations and you've overdelivered, you are my favorite influencer for at least seventy-two hours. But don't just make a generic request. This is where research and strategy are key. When everyone starts talking about Fashion Week, tell the advertiser you'd love to be their correspondent and you'll include an item of clothing or a beauty product in X number of photos throughout the week. If they have a semiannual sale coming up, suggest partnering with them a month before the sale to promote it to your followers and tease some of the great items that will be available. Take a look at some past activations the advertiser has done and figure out what you could bring to the table that will make it even better.

For even longer-term partnerships or the holy grail of brand ambassadorships, think about life events that your audience will care about. If you're going to spend the next year sprucing up your home, pitch that to Lowe's, Home Depot, or Wayfair and see if they'll be the official partner of your home renovation. In exchange for products and monetary compensation, you'll shop exclusively at their store while updating your home, and your audience will have a constant reminder that X advertiser is a great place to get everything they'll need. Pregnant? From the announcement that you're expecting to the first picture of your newborn baby, partner with a brand like Destination Maternity. They also have a partnership with buybuy BABY, so if the pregnancy partnership goes well, you'll be able to discuss a partnership during your first year as a new mom.

Bust out your media kit and add a new section detailing this partnership. Include the duration and how many blogs/vlogs they would get along with the number of Instagram posts. Write the headline and a summary of a few articles you would include as well as the overview of any contests or sweepstakes you would run. Let them know why this collaboration makes sense and why your audience will love it. Give them everything but the price. Too low and you'll sell yourself short. Too high and you'll price yourself out. You want to get them excited about the partnership because it will be mutually beneficial. You can hammer out the specifics later. And if you're worried about them stealing your idea, don't be. It's not necessarily the idea that is special. It's your aesthetic, your audience, and your vision. Don't think of it as why this idea would make a great campaign. Think about why *you* are the best person to execute it.

Constantly coming up with new ideas is exhausting, and no one knows your audience better than you do, so do your research, get creative, and pitch away. The brand and your audience will thank you for it.

THE COLLABORATION

A big day for any influencer is the day they secure a major collaboration with a brand. Jackie Aina (@jackieaina) is an influencer known for her commentary on the exclusionary practices of the beauty industry. For her thirtieth birthday she announced that she was teaming up with Too Faced Cosmetics to expand their Born This Way foundation line and create darker and deeper shades. Marianna Hewitt (@marianna_hewitt) is known for her rose-tinted Instagram feed, and she collaborated with NYC-based accessories brand Dagne Dover on a "personally curated capsule collection in warm shades of blush and dusk."

You've probably heard of Michelle Phan's Em Cosmetics company and Zoe Sugg's Zoella Beauty brand, but there are many influencers who have used their online success to create and market products. Shayla Mitchell has partnered with Maybelline, Jacklyn Hill has partnered with Morphe and Becca, and Carli Bybel has partnered with BH Cosmetics. Kathleen Fuentes has KL Polish, and Laura Lee created Laura Lee Los Angeles, a makeup line that is cruelty-free and vegan.

But you don't need to be a mega influencer to try your hand at collaborations. There are plenty of smaller brands that would *love* to collaborate with an influencer who will promote a co-branded product. Spend time looking for small skincare/makeup/perfume companies and clothing/accessories designers. Just like you would put together a pitch for a brand for a long-term partnership, create a proposal for collaborating with this brand. What expertise or special skills can you offer? How do you know this will resonate with your audience? Why are you the best person for this partnership? Wow business owners with your knowledge of their industry and the research you've done on their brand and their goals.

Networking is key. Whether you're building your community, packaging your brand, monetizing your influence, or planning your future, networking is the common thread that runs through all stages of influence.

EXPERT TIP

The basic formula for influence is *P* × *N*: Persuasiveness times Network. If you're reading this book and you want to be or already are an influencer, then the chances are you intuitively understand how this formula works better than ninety-nine out of a hundred people. Even if you have just five or ten thousand followers, then you already have a network. And if you're not there yet, you can get there. Wherever you are on this journey, you know the steps to take. You're the influencer and everyone else is not.

There are going to be haters along the way. They will be wrong, but some of them will manage to get under your skin. Just know this, and I can tell you with certainty having followed influencer marketing from the start, having talked with many influencers, and having talked to all types of industry insiders: The wind is at your back.

People are only just beginning to realize what influencers can be. The fact that you're an influencer now, at this moment, the beginning of it all, already suggests that you're favored. That favor will continue because influencer recognition is just getting started.

—Alexander H. Hennessy (@mralexanderhennessy), cofounder of CreatorsCollective

What I've outlined here may seem like lofty goals, but remember, every single influencer you see achieving great success started with zero followers, including all of our icons. They had to make mistakes and learn the hard way. Not only do you have their career paths to draw inspiration from, but you also have this book to guide you. If you are starting now, you may think you are late to the party, but you're wrong. There are still thousands of brands trying to figure out influencer marketing and hundreds more spending millions of dollars each year on campaigns. You're fighting for a piece of the pie, but that pie is only getting bigger. Let's get to work!

INFLUENCER ICON

SONA GASPARIAN

@sonagasparian + simplysona.com

Sona is a class act, and every time I've worked with her, my coworkers and clients have always been impressed. She has a knack for connecting with her audience, and her beauty school background and experience as a professional makeup artist probably have a little bit to do with that. She has her own cosmetics line, Pérsona Cosmetics (available at personacosmetics.co or at Ulta), and this is just the beginning. Her brand may be Simply Sona, but there's nothing simple about her.

ON CHOOSING YOUR BLOG NAME . . .

This was one of the hardest decisions for me, I wanted the name of my blog to be very welcoming and approachable rather than intimidating and too editorial. I wanted my blog to be a place where everyday women could get helpful tips on beauty, fashion, and lifestyle. I named it Simply Sona because it sounds very friendly, inviting, and relatable, which is key.

Simply Sona can evolve with me as I grow into different stages of my life. Although my expertise is in beauty, I wanted to share other aspects of my life with my readers. I share fashion posts because I'm 5' 2" (on a good day) and sharing styling tips with my petite followers is super fun. The reason why I decided to add a lifestyle section to my blog is because that's where I connect with my readers on a more personal level.

Sundays with Sona is a series where I chat about my struggles. I've shared personal stories from being an immigrant trying to fit in, to struggling with severe acne. You'd be surprised how many women relate to my story and feel more connected to me. I don't want people to look at my blog or Instagram feed and think, *Wow, her life is perfect.* I want people to know that I'm human with my own imperfections and insecurities.

ON YOUR INSTAGRAM CHANNEL . . .

I used to be so picky about my Instagram and making sure my feed was super curated, but I've completely changed that. I think nowadays, people are looking for more genuine content. I even realized that I was tired of the curated feeds; I'd much rather see honest posts. I balance that by sharing high-quality images that are relatable. I don't spend as much time on fancy flat lays as I used to because I don't think it's realistic to have your makeup lay so perfectly.

As for sponsored content, I always make sure my followers are taking something away from it. For example, if I'm promoting a hairspray, I'll make sure to give people tips on how to style a certain hairstyle rather than just say how much I love the hairspray. I ask myself, "What value am I offering my followers with this image?" This helps me come up with creative concepts that will benefit my followers as well as the brand.

ON HAVING A GREAT ON-CAMERA PRESENCE . . .

I think professionalism comes with preparation, and I always overprepare myself for projects that I get hired for. When I first started on YouTube four years ago, I was so shy and afraid to be myself in front of the camera. I sounded like a robot that was sharing beauty tips and tricks. I honestly don't think I made personal connections with my viewers until I became more comfortable being myself. That's why my most important tip is to be yourself while still being professional.

When I film, regardless if the content is branded or not, I'm 100 percent authentic. If you drop a brush or mispronounce something, roll with it and correct yourself. You don't need to cut it out of the video. People are able to connect with you a lot more if you show who you really are.

ON GROWING AS A PROFESSIONAL . . .

I attended makeup school because I wanted to be a professional makeup artist. YouTube wasn't around for me back then. Going to makeup school gave me more confidence, but looking back, it didn't really teach me much. I gained most of my knowledge from working at MAC and being a freelance makeup artist.

During my time as a makeup artist, I became familiar with different skin tones and textures, so I've really learned what works for some people, and what doesn't. Having this experience helps me share knowledgeable tips with my audience. I don't think going to beauty school is necessary, especially now when you can learn everything on platforms like YouTube. I do think that practice makes perfect, so working at a counter is probably the best way to learn and perfect the craft.

ON WORKING WITH YOUR SIGNIFICANT OTHER . . .

KB (my husband) is a huge part of the Simply Sona brand. When I first started, I was with an MCN (multi-channel network) and my manager was working with thirty other channels. I got frustrated and eventually left because my emails would get ignored. KB stepped in and managed all of my incoming inquiries from brands that wanted to work with me. It was great because we made personal connections with all the brands without the "middleman."

I recently signed with a well-known agency (one of the worst decisions of my career) and after one year, I left. At the end of the day, it's tough finding the right team to represent you and your brand integrity in this new frontier. It's a new industry and some players may overlook its intricacies and only focus on the lucrative side of the business.

My best advice on working with a spouse or significant other is to set boundaries and designate responsibilities. We *try* to avoid talking about work after 7 P.M. every day.

ON DEALING WITH HATERS . . .

In this business, I learned to keep my head down and do my own thing. I'm friendly with everyone, but I don't allow myself to get too close because I've been hurt before. Unfortunately, there is jealousy in every industry and my industry is no exception. As for hateful comments from the public, I'm fortunate to have a very mature audience. I tend to just get constructive criticism from my subscribers, which I really appreciate.

ON TAKING IT TO THE NEXT LEVEL . . .

I launched Pérsona Cosmetics in December 2016 with the help of my husband. Before social media, the dream of having my own cosmetics line felt too big, but I quickly realized that no dream is too big. I truly felt like I had something different to offer in the beauty space.

For our first product, I launched a neutral eyeshadow palette designed specifically for brown eyes. There may be hundreds of neutral palettes, but there is nothing like this in the market—a palette especially designed to enhance brown eyes. The success of our first product was truly remarkable, I still get emotional reading all the reviews and feedback from our customers.

One of the biggest beauty stores, Ulta Beauty, noticed the positive reviews and picked up the Identity Palette. Cool, right? Since then, we've grown our brand and are in development stages for multiple products to launch in 2018.

We'll see what the future holds, but I know that I'm just getting started. Each year, I'm going to continue to work harder to make my dreams come true, while hopefully raising a family. I think it's very important to dream big, but it's most important to set goals to achieve them. Dreams are nothing if you don't take the necessary actions to make them a reality. Set realistic goals toward your dreams and cross them off the list, one task at a time. It's also important to surround yourself with a team of people who believe in your vision and want to be a part of your journey.

ON WOMEN DOMINATING INFLUENCER MARKETING . . .

I think it's great that so many women became successful entrepreneurs from platforms like Instagram and YouTube. I do think that most influencers, including myself, can sometimes set unrealistic goals for women by posting edited photos, but I also believe that people are now educated on the various apps we use to edit them.

A lot of influencers are open about their editing techniques, and I even shared an entire post on how I edit my Instagram photos and the filters I use to create a cohesive color scheme. My readers really appreciated this because it gave them an insight into how I create my content, which keeps it real. Finding the sweet spot between overediting and raw content is key. Without editing, you wouldn't have visually compelling imagery. I would tell people who aspire to be content creators to be true to themselves while still producing quality content.

ON HINDSIGHT BEING 20/20 . . .

Early on, I wish I knew to be myself and open up more to my viewers. Also, I wish I was more consistent with my content. The market is so saturated now that you have to be consistent and set yourself apart from everyone. The advice I have for aspiring influencers is to not overthink things. Although I think equipment (camera, lighting, microphone, etc.) is important, there are many other things that play a role in the success of your channel.

You really need to find what you can offer to your viewers that is different. It can be something small, like creating a channel in a different language or having a unique intro. Be yourself and make connections with people.

Conclusion

"Why not me?" is the question I have asked myself more than any other. Even if it's something as small as entering a raffle for a free lunch if you drop your business card into a fishbowl, I always say to myself, "They have to pick someone, why not me?" I think above all else, that's the reason why I've had such an exciting and successful career. More than having the right degree, or making the right connections, three simple words are the reason why you are holding this book in your hands right now: Why. Not. Me?

They say men will apply for a job if they feel like they can do 60 percent of the work listed on the job description, but women need to feel like they can do 100 percent of the work before they put themselves out there. This is crazy talk and no way to get ahead in the world. I have had four "real" jobs during my professional career and I wasn't 100 percent ready for any of them. Why take a job if you're not going to learn? To stretch? To grow? Sure there might be someone more qualified than I was also in the running, but I've always been qualified enough, I'm a fast learner, and I work hard. They have to hire someone, why not me?

This mantra pretty much explains how this book was born. I was thinking someone ought to write a book that explains how this whole influencer marketing thing works because people are out here acting like they have no idea what's going on. Someone ought to write a book, why not me?

After "why not me" there are three other submantras, if you will, that have changed my life.

The first is *Say yes and figure out the details later.* In 2011, I was offered the chance of a lifetime to serve as a North American ambassador for Nivea's 100th anniversary. They were going to send me to Germany for three days to hang out on a cruise ship with Rihanna. They were going to pay me and all I needed to do was tweet about it. One small problem: I was offered this gig on Monday, I was leaving on Wednesday, and I did not have a passport.

But when they asked me if I could go did I say no? Of course not. I said I will be there. I immediately started freaking out because I had never had a passport and didn't even know if you could get one in 48 hours, but it turns out you could. Not only did I have the best time, but I also met a friend on that trip who was there on behalf of her PR firm. She later started working at Hearst and recommended me to my future boss. That job led to the writing of this book. Imagine where I'd be if I had said no?

The second is *Ask for forgiveness not permission.* When I first started my blog, I knew I was going to need to make actual money from it if it was ever going to be a full-time thing. I didn't really have any options, so I decided I was going to fake it until I made it. I had seen banner ads for *The Real Housewives of New York* on another blog I followed and I saved them and put them on my own site. Forget that banner ads have tracking codes and I was probably ruining someone's calculations. I was giving the show free press. What's the worst that could happen? They realize they're not paying me for those ads and ask me to take them down?

That didn't happen, but you know what did? An ad campaign with Svedka for thousands of dollars. They hadn't seen any advertising on my site before the *Housewives* ads, so they weren't sure if I was accepting placements. This buy came right as I was deciding if I was going to stay in law school or try my hand at this whole digital content thing. I dropped out a few months later.

The third is *Give freely and don't hesitate.* Not many people know this, but my husband and I got engaged on our first date. Now, we knew of each other beforehand, we were in the same section in law school, but we weren't friends. One night after work, I decided to take the long way to the train—it was a perfect summer night for a walk—when I ran into him on the sidewalk.

What could have been a quick and awkward small talk moment turned into a 6-hour conversation where we talked about everything from our relationships with our parents and how many kids we wanted to have to our greatest ambitions and why we were still single.

I went home later that night thinking I had blown my chance with him because women are supposed to be mysterious and there was definitely no mystery left. But the next night, when my friend cancelled on me and I needed a plus one for an event I was covering, I asked him to come along. Before the date was over he looked me right in the eyes and said, "I know what I want, and I'm not one to beat around the bush. I think we should get married." And I said "Okay!" We did wait two years before walking down the aisle, but if I had been more reserved when I bumped into him or hesitated when he laid it all out on the line for me, I'd probably have ended up like Ryan Gosling's character in *La La Land*.

If you meet someone who is in a position to help you achieve a goal, don't hold back. If you run into a writer who covers your vertical, tell her you would be forever grateful if she included you in her next influencer roundup. If you're at a conference with your favorite influencer, tell her you'd love to collaborate with her. If you meet the influencer director for your favorite brand, tell her you want to become her brand ambassador and ask how you can make that happen. Make each and every conversation count and never walk away wishing you would have said more or done more. It won't always work out, but the only way to get what you want is to go for it.

Now that we have some feel-good stories under our belt, and are ready to dive headfirst into the pool of opportunity, let's tackle the three big tasks you'll need to complete if you want to go all in on this journey to becoming a full-time influencer.

1. **Be a vlogger, a blogger, and an Instagram star.** Is it hard to edit videos? Yes. Is it hard to consistently write compelling content? Yes. Is it hard to build and maintain an engaged community on Instagram? Yes. Is it extremely hard to do all three? Yes. And that's exactly why you are going to do it. If you can speak on camera, write, and connect with people online, brands will be lining up to work with you. It may take you longer to perfect all three and you might grow at a slower pace than some of your peers, but you will outlast them all. Someone has to be a triple-threat influencer . . . why not you?

2. **Spend time thinking about your hot-button issue.** Plenty of people want

women to be able to look great on a budget, and while that beat may have worked in 2009, it won't fly in 2018. I'm not saying you need to be controversial, but you need to find an angle that keeps you up at night. When you are working a full-time job and creating content in your spare time, nighttime is where all your magic will happen. Don't pick a topic that will put you to sleep.

Iskra Lawrence (@iskra) hated that people photoshopped her body, so her entire platform focuses on body acceptance. Heidi Nazarudin (@theambitionista) didn't understand why the world thought that being a businesswoman meant you had no style, so she created a community for the corporate go-getter. Olya Hill (@livingnotes) wanted to show the world that you can be a retired ballerina with seven kids and still be killing it. Jackie Aina (@jackieaina) wanted to make videos for girls who looked like her and didn't think mainstream sites understood that dark-skinned women were beautiful too.

Think back to a time someone underestimated you or looked down on you and it filled you with rage. They thought you couldn't do something you were capable of. Tap into that and let it direct your spin on lifestyle content. Someone has to be the voice of your issue . . . why not you?

3. **Write down your biggest goal and work backward.** There are influencers who are now actresses and singers. They have fashion collections and beauty lines. Their YouTube shows are now television shows and motion pictures. Their paths may be different, but you know what they all have in common? They all started with zero subscribers, zero page views, and zero followers.

   Many people think they're afraid of failure, but they're actually afraid of success. Afraid of what will happen if that brand does agree to their proposal or if that website does run a profile on them. Success can quickly turn your life upside down, but if you plan for it, you will be prepared. Someone has to build an empire . . . why not you?

AND THAT'S ALL SHE WROTE

The contents of this book have given you the foundation you'll need to succeed in the world of influencer marketing. Whether you're still building a community, learning to package your brand, or finally monetizing your influence, you are now prepared to leap over any obstacles that may attempt to block your path. Go forth, conquer, and create. Someone has to be part of the next wave of influencer icons . . . why not you?

GLOSSARY

The amount of lingo you have to be hip to continues to amaze me. You may be an influencer, but you're dealing with people who speak legalese, corporate slang, and other dialects of the English language. I present to you, the Glossary.

Advertiser—the brand calling all the shots. They have the money and they make the rules.

Agency—a group working on behalf of the advertiser. They can be a media agency, a creative agency, or a public relations agency. Sometimes they have the money, so they can make some of the rules, but they still have to answer to the Advertiser.

Agent—someone who represents an influencer. Her job is to make sure the influencer makes money. She only gets paid if the influencer gets paid, so her motto is ABC—always be closing.

Ambassador—an influencer who is working with a brand on a long-term contract. An ambassador is essentially the "face" of a brand during her ambassadorship. An influencer can be an ambassador for a certain period of time (2018, Fall 2018), an event season (Fashion Week, back-to-school), or for a particular product (mascara, denim line, anti-frizz shampoo).

Approvals—a period of time where everyone and their mom needs to look over the content and give it the green light. This is also known as the CYA (cover your ass) period.

Article—a piece of content that usually has a lot of text and pictures to break them up. This is usually a profile of an influencer.

BCE—stands for branded content editor. This person works at a publisher and is in charge of coming up with the details of the branded content. She also looks at all the influencers to make sure they are "on brand."

Bio—the two to three lines on your Instagram profile where you squeeze in as much information about yourself as possible. Also, the page on your website where you give the reader more details on your story and the type of content you'd like to create.

Bluehost—a web host. It holds all the files for your website. Bluehost is my favorite because it's easy to navigate around its site, it's inexpensive, and its customer service is really good for when you accidentally break your code or delete your site.

Brand—oftentimes used interchangeably with "advertiser," but at Hearst it means one of our in-house titles like *Cosmopolitan* or *Seventeen*.

Brand Affinity—a fancy word to show compatibility between an influencer and an advertiser/brand. If you're an influencer and 50 percent of your followers follow a certain beauty brand, that is a very high affinity. The bigger this number is, the better.

Brief—the document you receive from the advertiser, agency, or brand that provides guidelines on creating content. It will tell you what hashtags to use, what handles to mention, the tone of the content, and other valuable pieces of information.

Budget—how much money someone has to pay you. People think a very popular brand will always have a large budget, but that's not true. Budgets vary, so always keep an open mind.

Call Sheet—a document you'll receive ahead of a photo or video shoot. It will include where the shoot will be held, who will be on set, the schedule of the day, and other important details.

Call Time—the time you will be expected on set. It is included in the call sheet.

Campaign—the project you are a part of. It will have a specific start and end time.

Casting Call—when looking for talent, also known as casting, a casting director may set up a date and time and try to see as many influencers as possible during that window.

Category Exclusivity—if an advertiser asks for this it means you cannot work with any competitors in the same category. Popular categories include beauty products (mascara, lipstick, foundation) alcohol/spirits (vodka, tequila, rum), and accessories (watches, handbags, sunglasses).

Celebrity—an influencer whose fame is attributed to her offline career. For the most part, people are following her on social media because they are a fan of her movies, music, TV shows, or sports team.

Circle Back—a complicated way of saying, "I'll get back to you." I absolutely HATE IT when people say this, but I say it all the time. When in Rome . . .

Client—the person who is giving you money. You have to make this person happy or she will take your money away.

COB—stands for close of business. If someone needs something by COB, it usually means by 6 P.M. Keep in mind that may be EST if she's in New York or PST if she's in Los Angeles.

Competitor—a company that the advertiser is up against when consumers are choosing which product to buy. Some advertisers are very realistic about their competitors. Others, not so much.

Connect Offline—conference call speak that means "We'll talk about this when the call is over."

Content—photos, videos, and text being created for a social media platform.

Content Creator—someone who makes photos, videos, and text for social media platforms.

Contract—an agreement between the advertiser/agency/brand and the influencer that includes the campaign information and the deliverables.

CPC—stands for cost per click. If an advertiser pays you to drive traffic to their website, the amount they've paid you divided by the number of clicks is the CPC.

CPV—stands for cost per view. When doing video campaigns there is a price per view if an advertiser is running an ad on social media. Advertisers like to compare traditional CPVs to an influencer's CPV so they will divide how much they paid you by how many views your video received to determine that number.

Deck—a PowerPoint or Keynote presentation that marketers HATE creating, but have to for advertisers. It usually has campaign ideas, influencer pitches, and pricing.

Deliverables—what you are responsible for producing (photos/video/text) and publishing (blog posts, videos, photos).

Disclaimer—a note to give people important information that they would like to know. You usually will see one of these on a blog that says, "Some of the links you see are affiliate links and we will receive monetary compensation if you click and buy."

DocuSign—an app that lets you electronically sign documents, because the days of printing, signing, and scanning are over.

Engagement—the number of likes, comments, retweets, shares, and repins your content receives.

Engagement Rate—the number of followers divided by the number of engagements you have on one post or the last ten to twelve posts.

EOD—stands for end of day. This is usually 12 A.M. in the time zone of the person who is sending it. But it really means "have it in my inbox by the time I look at it tomorrow."

EOW—stands for end of week. It usually means the person asking you for something would like it on Friday so that it will be in her inbox when she comes into work on Monday morning. This is also usually assuming the person won't be working on the weekend.

Exclusivity—a term referring to the amount of time you are prohibited from working with competitors.

Facebook Live—a video that is recorded and streams in real time on Facebook.

Filter—an overlay on a photo/video that changes how it looks.

Flat Lay—when you lay items flat and take a photo of them. This can be an outfit or things you're packing in a suitcase, gym bag, or diaper bag. A "bag spill" can be considered a type of flat lay.

Flight—the length of a campaign or the length of time content has to be live/remain visible on your site.

FTC—stands for Federal Trade Commission. Their job is to make sure consumers are not deceived. They're pretty much the #ad police.

Gallery—one piece of content that you can scroll through for multiple images/videos. Can be used on a blog, Instagram, or Facebook post.

Glam Squad—people who provide hair, makeup, and styling for a photo shoot.

Go-see—a term frequently used in modeling and increasingly in influencer marketing where an individual goes to see a casting director so the director can see how the individual looks in real life.

Hashtag—the "#" sign used on social media. When attached to a word the term created strings together every status update that uses it so you can follow the conversations. You cannot put punctuation or spaces in a hashtagged term. You'd think some people would have learned this lesson by now, but alas, many have not.

Haul/Anti-Haul—a type of YouTube video where you go to a store and show your audience all the things you bought. An anti-haul is relatively new in comparison and is when an influencer states all the things she will never buy.

Influencer—someone who has influence. For the purposes of social media, that influence must be online.

KPI—stands for key performance indicators. This refers to the metrics that will show you if a campaign is successful. Common KPIs include impressions, engagements, video views, clicks, time on site, purchases, downloads, etc.

Lifecaster—someone who broadcasts her life on Instagram but doesn't create content the way a content creator does. She's pretty much living her life and being fabulous, and documenting the process, and her audience is loving up.

Listicle—content displayed in a list form: "Five Ways to Wear This Dress" or "Nine Things to Pack for a Trip to Europe."

Manager—someone who provides career direction for an influencer. She can also pitch and book an influencer for campaigns if the influencer doesn't have an agent.

Mention—calling out the name of an advertiser or brand on social media by using the "@" symbol.

Mood Board—a visual representation of a shoot to be approved by a brand. The mood board could include inspiration of the location, clothing, makeup, hair, poses, and style. Think of it as a giant Pinterest board.

O&O—stands for owned and operated. This is usually seen on a contract in the usage section and means the content can be used on any site the advertiser/brand owns and operates like a website, blog, or social channels.

Publicist—a person in charge of your public relations. Her job pretty much entails dealing with the press and making sure you have a positive image. She also handles damage control if you make a big mistake.

Redline—used by lawyers when they edit a contract. Contracts are usually written in Microsoft Word and when you make edits to it, redlines are created to show where changes were made.

Retail—a physical location. Usually refers to a store when an advertiser is describing usage. If it includes retail, that means they can put your photos up in the store as a general poster or highlighting the product you were promoting.

ROI—stands for return on investment. When an advertiser spends $1 and gets $1 back, the ROI is 1:1. Influencer marketing tends to have a higher ROI than traditional advertising, unless the wrong influencer is cast. Then you can have what I call negative ROI.

Rolling Lunch—when you're on set sometimes there is an official lunch break, but other times they bring out lunch and you eat when you have a break. The latter is a rolling lunch.

Roster—a list of clients a talent agency represents. Also the list of influencers pitched to an advertiser for a campaign.

Sentiment—how someone feels after reading your content. Are they happy, sad, angry, etc.?

SOW—this stands for scope of work. It lays out what you're hired to do.

Tag—when you're creating organic content and you want the brand to take note, but you don't want to mention them.

Takeover—When you post three Instagram posts in a row, essentially letting the advertiser "take over" the top row of your feed.

Tutorial—a YouTube video where you teach your audience how to do something.

Usage—how the content created for a campaign will be used/where it will appear.

Vertical—a category like style, beauty, fitness, travel, home decor, DIY, etc.

Wordpress—a platform used by most bloggers.

Acknowledgments

Wow. Dreams really do come true. I am a published author! This is so exciting. It's also very dangerous, because anytime someone questions my authority on influencer marketing, my new retort will be "Fine, don't listen to me. It's not like I wrote a book about it or anything." But seriously, there are so many people to thank.

First and foremost, my husband. Thank you, Alexander, for telling me to write this book. And pushing me to write the proposal. And bothering me until I sent it out. And taking our son out on mini-trips so that I could complete the manuscript under the insane deadline I placed upon myself. And making sure the book lived up to my expectations. And being incredibly supportive of my career. And being the kind of husband and father only found in unrealistic movies. My life completely changed the day I met you, and you are my everything.

I could not continue without thanking Barbara Baez-Meister, my right-hand woman. This book would not have been completed without you holding down the fort at Hearst while I took off many days to write it. You've been with me for six years through multiple jobs and countless side-hustles and you're more than just a colleague, you're family. Started from the bottom, now we're here!

I also need to thank: Jade Sherman for introducing me to my agent, Steve Ross, providing quotes for this book, and hooking me up with the amazing Teni Panosian. Steve Ross at Abrams Artists Agency, for working diligently to find the right publisher for this book, because so many people just did not get the influencer marketing phenomenon. Denise Silvestro, for being a fantastic editor who really understood the vibe I was going for and held my hand this entire time. Michelle Addo, Vida Engstrand, Claire Hill, and the entire Kensington family, for believing in this book and making sure people know to buy it.

Jacqueline Deval, for telling me that my proposal was special. You publish Queen Oprah's books, so this was the best compliment I could hope to receive! Alexandra Carlin, for always being so interested and invested in my success at Hearst. Allison Keane and Liv Ren, for helping me with all PR and media-related things. Lee Sosin, Laura Kalehoff, and Keri Hansen, for helping me grow as a professional. Sam Gladis, for being my number-one fan and always letting me rant (and occasionally rave) in her office.

Alexandra Pereira, Alyssa Bossio, Cara Santana, Heidi Nazarudin, Joy Cho, Sazan Hendrix, Sona Gasparian, and Teni Panosian, for taking time out of their insanely busy schedules to provide wisdom and inspiration to my readers. Brittany Xavier, Cynthia Andrew, Iskra Lawrence, Jeanne Grey, Jenny Tsang, Jessamyn Stanley, Jessica Franklin, Krystal Bick, Olya Hill, Renee Hahnel, and Tania Sarin, for providing insights that only come from playing this game and playing it well. Beca Alexander, Chloe Watts, Hannah Kluckhohn, India-Jewel Jackson, Jada Wong, Jane Lim, Jennifer Tzeses, Jessy Grossman, Maximilian Ulanoff, and Rana Zand, for dropping gems from the business side and providing access to your fabulous clients.

My mom, for keeping the first book I ever wrote, in the first grade, about a dancing baby who moved her crib around the room. Mike Mathewson and Carolyn Landis, for being my best friends, reading my proposal, and buying my book even though I would have given them a free copy. Zlata Faerman, for being a constant source of positive energy.

Everyone who has ever attended a CreatorsCollective event, all of my friends/followers on Facebook, Instagram, and LinkedIn, for asking questions that would guide this book, and every single person who read this far, because that is dedication!

Finally, I don't show it enough, but I am thankful to God for waking me up every morning and putting all these wonderful people and opportunities in my life, and giving me the gift of communication. I can't wait to see what else you have in store for me.